All Originality Makes A Dull Church

All Originality
Makes A
Dull Church

Dan Baumann

VISION HOUSE PUBLISHERS
Santa Ana, California 92705

Copyright © 1976 by Vision House Publishers
Santa Ana, California 92705

Library of Congress Catalogue Number 75-42852
ISBN 0-88449-053-X

Printed in the United States of America

45, 365

*To Roy and Ebba Baumann
With much appreciation from a son
who
learned to love Christ and the church
through their godly example.*

Contents

Contents

A Note to the Reader

I am indebted to a number of people for the production of this volume: Mrs. Elaine Quade, in the midst of her duties as my personal secretary, did some of the original typing and regulated my schedule to allow this work to become a reality. Miss Janet Gruehl, a member of our congregation, gave much appreciated advice regarding style. And, as always, "friend wife" Nancy played an important part. Not only did she provide continual inspiration through the project, but she typed the final two drafts of the manuscript. These three friends deserve much of the praise for any virtue this volume contains. I accept sole responsibility for its errors in fact or its weaknesses in evaluation. Thanks are also in order to the Bethel Seminary family, St. Paul, Minnesota, for allowing me to test these ideas in a week-long lectureship on Church Growth in October, 1975.

Introduction

I LOVE THE CHURCH; always have! My love affair began as a boy attending the Moody Church in Chicago. Week after week I sat with four thousand other worshipers and heard the Scriptures expounded by Dr. Harry Ironside. It was both instructive and inspirational. I loved it!

When I got into my teens, we moved to a small neighborhood church, a step undertaken when a pastor friend with a warm heart and a cold church enlisted my parents' support. Then and there my mother and father caught a vision for ministering in a church that had aching needs; a place where they were really needed. They worked, they taught, and they prayed until at length that church came alive with the refreshing touch of God's Spirit. My involvement, however, as a high-school student was minimal. I would typically fidget, read bulletin inserts, scan the take-home papers, and doodle during the worship services. Dad had had about enough of that. One Sunday he squeezed my knee and said, "Dan, pay attention." After the service was over he informed me that I had to take notes on the sermons.

From that day to the present I have taken notes on just about every sermon I have heard. And you know, of course, what happened—the preaching improved. My appreciation for the ministry of the Word and the task of the church began to soar.

Bible institute, college, seminary, and graduate school confirmed my feelings. I took a New England church, and what a choice group of Christians they were. They feigned interest in my preaching, smiled at my humor, endured my administrative naiveté, and never ceased to encourage their fledgling parson. Bless their patient, gracious hearts! Little did they know they were fostering a love affair in the heart of one very grateful and terribly green pastor.

I spent the next eight years teaching in our denominational seminary. With the exception of the antarctic climate of Minnesota, it was exhilarating to the spirit. When I wasn't in the classroom, I was in the pulpit. Nine interim pastorates during those years convinced me that the "action is in the church."

For the last three years, I have shared a beautiful pilgrimage with a new congregation in Whittier, California. Its overwhelming response has further intensified my love for the church. I have never loved it more than I do today. It has fantastic possibilities. After all, the church has been God's chosen instrument of blessing for nineteen hundred years. It has a great "track record."

As we look back over the last two and one-half decades, we discover that the American church has been the recipient of both cursing and eulogy. During the '50s and early '60s the debunkers were having a field day. It was fashionable to take pot shots at "God's frozen people" who were comfortably settled into their "suburban captivity." Friends of the church brought out its dirty linen, while the enemies of the church panned it unmercifully. It was all rather messy.

Well, the church lived through that curious time, and before long we were caught up in the onrush of the renewal movement—a time of affirmation, experimentation, and revitalization. Once again, it was a joyful time for the church. Now, in the '70s, we are in the midst of another era, namely, the church growth movement. The success stories are sufficient to boggle the mind. Ironically, while many churches are experiencing a decline in interest, attendance, and finances, thousands of sanctuaries are bursting at the seams. Books are being written, seminars are being conducted, and Christians are buzzing everywhere.

What is the secret of growing churches? You get different answers from everybody—a bus ministry, body life, the return to expository preaching, superaggressive leadership, or soul-winning. Which answer is right? There probably is no wrong answer. My chief concern is that what is right for one congregation may not be right for another. The dilemma many face is simply this—we want to grow, but how? What do *we* do? Which model do *we* follow? Who has an answer for *our* church?

This volume is an attempt to sift through the success stories and place the growing churches into manageable categories where they may be studied. My hope is that this approach will unveil some useful insights for your consideration and implementation. Growth is a biblical idea and is, in most situations, the will of God. If we have Good News, it is a sin to keep it from anyone.

Alan R. Tippett, in *Church Growth and the Word of God,* says,

The attitude that we must expect slow growth distresses me. It is quite foreign to the New Testament, which, on the contrary, has a rich range of picturesque imagery that shows growth is to be expected—both physical, numerical growth from outside and spiritual, qualitative growth from within. The New Testament nouns and verbs leave no room for static causes.

Note the following metaphors:

(1) quantitative imagery (catching fish—Matt. 13:47, 48; bread under influence of leavening—Matt. 13:33)
(2) imagery of ingathering (harvest—John 4:35; prayer for harvesters—Matt. 9:37, 38)
(3) imagery of incorporation (bringing folks to a banquet—Luke 14:21-24)
(4) organic imagery (growing seed becoming a mighty tree—Matt. 13:31, 32)
(5) imagery of penetration (light—John 8:12; 9:5)

While numerical growth is not the only way to determine vitality, it is *one* valid way (see Acts 2:41, 47; 6:1, 7; 11:21; 16:5).

It is my conviction that a static church is unhealthy because it is unbiblical. Whether you are a layman or a cleric, this volume is dedicated to you and your church as God's chosen instruments for blessing our world. May your church be alive and well for your good and God's glory.

FOR ADDITIONAL READING

Gerber, Vergil. *God's Way to Keep a Church Going and Growing*. Glendale, Calif.: Regal Books Division, G/L Publications, 1973.

McQuilkin, J. Robertson. *Measuring the Church Growth Movement*. Chicago: Moody Press, 1973.

Tippett, Alan R. *Church Growth and the Word of God*. Grand Rapids, Mich.: William B. Eerdmans Publishing Company, 1970.

Guiding Principles 1

1

Guiding Principles

At the outset of this study of church growth models, it is necessary to establish some useful guidelines in order to maximize the experience.

Be a Gleaner. Lessons learned by any local fellowship of believers ought to be common property of the entire body of Christ. Not to learn by the lessons of others is a waste of time and energy. A number of years ago there was a comedian on the Jack Paar show. He told of visiting friends in a quaint, rural community in New Hampshire. After dinner his host took him up to the attic to show off a fantastic machine that he had developed. He pushed a button, and an arm swung over and left an imprint. He pushed another button, and yet another arm swung over and left an imprint. The comedian smiled, rehearsed the scene one more time, then told Paar, "This poor fellow had reinvented the typewriter."

We have sometimes done the very same thing in the church. Why should the precious time that God has given us be used in *re*discovering that which is *already* the property of the body of Christ? Is it necessary that every form of ministry be home-grown, home-fed, and home-developed? Isn't it logical for the church, with its magnificent task and its sometimes limited resources, to avail itself of every lesson and truth it can muster? It is sad that the only lesson some learn from history is that we do not learn from history. As a concerned churchman, I am sure you want God's best for the ministry of Christ in your own neighborhood. The lessons learned in Texas may prove fruitful in Maine, Georgia, Utah, or in your church. No church should start from scratch. The pool of effectiveness is available to quench the thirst of many parched churches.

Charles Spurgeon said, "All originality and no plagiarism makes dull preaching." He was right. No man has a corner on the truth. The Holy Spirit has blessed churches in many localities with a very special touch from his sovereign hand. If God is doing something in another community which could also happen in your community, learn what you can about that success, glean from it the transferable concepts, and maybe the fire of heaven will fall afresh—this time on your church and your community. It can and does happen. Thousands of churches testify to the increased usefulness and expanded ministries that they enjoy today because they found a stimulus, a lesson, a principle, a program, a method, or an attitude in another location that God has used in their own situation. Be a gleaner. Take whatever you can from wherever you find it, and use it, assuming, of course, that it is transferable.

Be a Sociologist. Recently, after attending a church growth seminar at a "successful" West Coast church, a good friend asked, "How do you feel about sessions like that?" Before I had time to answer, he said that he felt frustrated to death. "Those things just won't work in our town." He was probably right. Success in one church cannot be easily transferred to another. In fact, what transforms one congregation, may kill another. Discernment is needed. If we are to benefit from the lessons of others, we need to become sociologists who glean the transferable concepts. Mark it well— much is *not* transferable from one setting to another. Principles which are crosscultural must be heeded with particular care. Programs are *not* absolutes; biblical principles are. Take care to distinguish one from the other.

A few examples may help clarify this concept. What works in an academic community like Palo Alto, California, may not work in a rural community. That is to say, the body-life service, popularized under the ministry of Pastor Ray Stedman, is dependent for its effectiveness upon a congregation of people who are accustomed to expressing themselves verbally with others. Those who are academically oriented have been actively participating in an environment where openness is the norm. Seventy percent of the body-life congregation (at Palo Alto on a Sunday night) is twenty-five years of age or younger. Therefore, when you attempt to bring body-life into a rural community where there has not been sufficient conditioning to share deep feelings in the presence of others, you may experience futility. When people have been passive in their worship experience and you insist that they "now share out of their gut," you will probably be frustrated by the response. You cannot transfer what works in one area into another without recognizing sociological, cultural, neighborhood expectations and conditioning that differ from community to community.

Consider another example. What works in a factory community may not work in a typical suburban community. Pastor Jack Hyles of the First Baptist Church in Hammond,

Indiana, has been eminently successful with a congregation of predominantly blue collar people. Literally thousands of pastors have gone to Hammond to participate in the Jack Hyles School. They return to their congregations full of enthusiasm and ideas. Frequently they meet resistance when they attempt to implement the ideas they have learned. The problem is that they have failed to reckon with a basic sociological reality—you cannot assume that Hammond success is universally applicable. More than one pastor has been exasperated with his white-collar members when they did not respond in the same way that folks responded to Hyles.

The thoughtful churchman must recognize a "homogeneous unit" in the Hammond setting. The manner of Hyles is authoritarian, which is compatible with the conditioning of factory workers who labor under the direction of foremen all week long. They need a foreman-type pastor to lead them. This style of leadership is destined to fail, however, in a congregation of professionals, executive types, and white-collar parishioners. What works in Hammond is fine for some, but not for everybody.

Peter Wagner of the Fuller Seminary faculty makes much of the "homogeneous unit" thesis in church growth philosophy. He maintains that growth occurs in the midst of groups that are distinguishable for their unity of approach, education, social standing, or the like. This thesis has much to commend it. The Church of the Saviour in Washington, D.C., is an excellent example. The members are very thoughtful types. Who is going to take five courses of twelve weeks each just to qualify for membership unless he is oriented in terms of inquisitiveness and study? That is a homogeneous unit.

Observe the ministry of the Penninsula Bible Church

(Palo Alto). It appears that the congregation is middle class or above and oriented toward higher education. This is not a value judgment; it is simply a matter of sociological classification. Programs are successes or failures based upon a number of factors, not the least of which is their adaptability to the group at hand. Community expectations are always worth noting. It has been more fashionable to attend church in the "Bible Belt" of America (predominantly the southeastern section of the states) than it has been in cities like New York or San Francisco. Community expectations are not uniform. Whether or not a program is transferable must be evaluated in the light of this reality. Approaches must be tailored to the community; thus, if two communities are similar, the ideas may be readily transferred. Every sociologically concerned Christian will give attention to at least the following important variables—education, age and sex profile, vocation, racial make-up, and local expectations. Concern for these items may be the difference between a ministry that flourishes and one that languishes.

Be an Innovator. Your greatest gift is you. God made you as a unique individual. Accept yourself as his child with gifts that are necessary for the health of the entire body of Christ. Reflect on the timely advice of Paul in Romans 12:3-6a, "For by the grace given to me I bid every one among you not to think of himself more highly than he ought to think, but to think with sober judgment, each according to the measure of faith which God has assigned him. For as in one body we have many members, and all the members do not have the same function, so we, though many are one body in Christ, and individually members one of another. Having gifts that differ according to the grace given to us, let us use them" (RSV). I have a concern that too quickly we can become

25

gleaners and not allow God to use our own unique contributions as men or women of God. Be both a gleaner and an innovator; share your own personality. If you have been a Christian for a number of years, you have much to share. God has been at work in your life. Acknowledge your worth as a Calvary-purchased gift to the church. It is false humility to assume that there should be two of anybody and not one of you. God knew what he was doing. You are terribly important. Allow your views to be expressed with that fresh touch of God the Spirit through you. Don't simply be a gleaner; be an innovator.

I frequently praise God for the innovation that exists in our church which has arisen because of the contributions of some of our nontheologically trained lay people. A salesman, one of the hardest working lay people I have ever met, gave our church the idea of offering two concurrent services on a Sunday morning. One service is traditional; the other is contemporary. Now our people can choose the type of service that ministers best to their needs. I never would have thought of it, but, thank God, Bob did! God can use you too. Be available!

The Soul-winning Church

2

2

The Soul-winning Church

SOUL-WINNING CHURCHES are growing churches. It is axiomatic that when people begin to share Christ, their church comes alive. New Christians become a continuing transfusion of "fresh blood" into the organism of the gathered community. This regular influx of converts is bound to create a dynamic situation.

Conversely, a church without an evangelistic emphasis tends to be a "maintenance ministry" (usually treading ecclesiastical water without making much progress) or a declining ministry (with both attendance and interest being adversely affected).

Two basic types of soul-winning churches have felt the invigorating touch of the Holy Spirit. The more traditional form focuses on a ministry *within the walls* of the church facilities. Here the programs are geared to drawing outsiders into the activities of the church. Once folks are within earshot of the buildings, they are confronted with the claims of Christ upon their lives. Both Sunday services and weekday activities are decision oriented. Worship services, Sunday school

29

classes, youth clubs and camps, even socials exist for the purpose of inviting people to trust Christ as Savior.

The other type of soul-winning church focuses its ministry *outside the walls*. Churches within this sector of Christendom use the buildings for worship and instruction; evangelism is geared to a ministry outside the buildings, within the community. The gathered church worships and studies; the dispersed church serves. Advocates of this emphasis remind us that we are to "go into all the world and preach the gospel" (Mark 16:15), *not* invite people "to jump into the pool of the church so that we might be fishers of men."

Both forms—within the walls and without the walls—have notable flourishing models. Each has much to commend it.

Within the Walls

Thomas Road Baptist Church
Lynchburg, Virginia

COMMUNITY

Lynchburg was founded in 1786 on the banks of the James River as a ferry crossing. Nestled in the foothills of the Blue Ridge Mountains, it is 50 miles northeast of Roanoke and 110 miles southwest of Richmond. It is a pleasant community with a moderate climate.

Through the years the town has moved away from the river to become a thriving city of 55,000, with an estimated 166,000 people living within a twenty-five-mile radius.

A wide range of industry and manufacturing concerns are found in the city. Products include shoes, foundry castings, paper, drugs, building materials, atomic reactors, electronic equipment, and custom-molded rubber products. A few large companies are represented—General Electric, Weyerhaeuser, Chap Stick, and the Mead Corporation.

Lynchburg is a "church town"; there is one church for every five hundred people. The flavor of religious life in this "Bible Belt" community is distinctively Protestant. There is only one Roman Catholic church in addition to a small Jewish synagogue among the 107 places of worship. On the other hand, there are eight Christian churches, nine Presbyterian, twenty Methodist, and no less than thirty-eight Baptist churches.

In summary, Lynchburg is a small, stable, lower-middle and middle class industrial community with a predominantly white, Protestant population.

CHURCH

Thomas Road Baptist Church, described by Elmer Towns as "the fastest growing church in America," was begun in June, 1956, when thirty-five adults and children gathered for the first meeting in the Mountain View Elementary School in Lynchburg. Jerry Falwell, a hometown boy, was its founding pastor.

On January 20, 1952, Falwell professed his faith in Christ at the Park Avenue Baptist Church of Lynchburg. It was a cold wintry evening when Garland Carey, an elderly white-haired gentleman, put his hand on Falwell's shoulder and said, "I'll go with you." They knelt at the altar together as the youth gave his life to the Savior. Instrumental in that decision was the week-in, week-out influence of the "Old Fashioned Revival Hour," to which Jerry's mother tuned in every week. The ministry of Charles Fuller was significant then, and it continues to this day. Falwell's broadcast has been consciously modeled after the Fuller pattern.

Falwell was an exceptional student. In grade school he had an "A" average, and in high school he was the valedictorian with a 98.6 average. A photographic memory served him well. He also excelled in sports. He was fullback and captain of the football team as a senior. The following summer he had a tryout with the St. Louis Cardinals' baseball team but left early to further his education. In college he captained the basketball team.

During his senior year at Baptist Bible College in Springfield, Missouri, he worked as an associate to Dr. Wendell Zimmerman of Kansas City Baptist Temple. Toward the end of the year, Zimmerman asked him to preach. Falwell was frightened to preach before seven to eight hundred people, but he asked God to give him a sign proving he was called into the ministry of the gospel. Nineteen people came forward at the invitation following his sermon on "Christ the Sanctifier" taken from Hebrews 10:10. The pattern was set. Jerry was called to preach for decisions.

The initial group of believers who gathered with Falwell in June, 1956, had left Park Avenue Baptist Church over local troubles. After the pastor of Park Avenue gave Jerry his approval, Falwell organized a church across town.

Immediately, the aggressive pastor began to broadcast on the radio and make plans for a growing church. Nothing seemed to stand in the way of his desire to build a great church. He worked fifty-two weeks a year, without vacation. He only sandwiched in one day or so a month for a physical reprieve. This pattern remains intact today.

"When the church started," Falwell said, "we thought that five hundred would make a large church, but when we reached five hundred, we found ourselves reaching for one thousand, then two thousand, next three thousand, and finally five thousand." He goes on to state, "I honestly believe we can average over ten thousand each Sunday in Thomas Road Baptist Church." Currently the membership is over fifteen thousand.

Success at the Thomas Road Baptist Church is attributable in large measure to the tireless effort of its pastor. Jerry Falwell practices and preaches "a super-aggressive local church" philosophy.

PROGRAM

Evangelism is at the heart of everything. It takes many avenues, but the purpose is the same—win people to faith in Christ. Their approach has been termed "Saturation evangelism.

The telephone. They will tear out all the pages from the local telephone book and assign a page each to members. In the following two or three weeks, they will call everybody on the list who is not a member of the church and invite them to come and hear their pastor preach on an interesting subject of importance to them. This contact is repeated again and again. If somebody is absent from Sunday school, he or she receives a phone call that week. Individuals are phoned even if they are gone for only one Sunday. The telephone is used as a means of drawing people into the church in order that they might be confronted with Christ. This continued interest pays off. As one man put it, "If you will stop bugging me, I will stop by!"

A bus ministry. A couple of things about this bus ministry need to be noted: First, they do not buy expensive buses. They purchase very reasonable buses and must, therefore, put almost as much into annual repairs on the bus as into the initial cost. I have been told that they will sometimes spend eight hundred dollars on the purchase and the average of eight hundred dollars on repairs in a single year. They do not take the buses on long trips or into the mountains; they are primarily used on Sunday school routes for the purpose of bringing people into the life of the local church.

Second, the bus captain is also the bus driver. He will go into a community and visit door to door, "We would like to stop by and pick up your children and bring them to our church." He develops a list early in the week. Then, on Saturday, he returns to double check to make sure that they will be there when he comes by. One hundred twenty-five buses go as far as fifty miles away to bring people to Thomas Road Baptist Church in Lynchburg. A superaggressive bus ministry has contributed much to their growing, dynamic local church. Hundreds have come to faith in Christ through this ministry.

Cassette tapes. Cassettes are made available for jail and hospital ministries. They are also sent to students, provided for guests, and available to the members of the church to share with their friends. Almost every Sunday-morning and evening message at Thomas Road Church is evangelistic. You are assured that if the message is recorded you can send it out and it will have an evangelistic appeal. That is their constant thrust.

Radio and TV. Thomas Road Baptist Church broadcasts daily on local radio. They feel it is more important to have once-a-day exposure than longer exposure once a week. It is a "low-sell" type of program—conversational in tone with musical requests honored, questions answered, and a brief devotional presented. Again and again throughout the program, listeners are invited to visit the church. Evangelism is geared to the local facilities.

Even the national television ministry invites people to visit Thomas Road Baptist Church for seminars and particular emphases that are hosted throughout the year at the church.

Publicity. This church has purchased sophisticated equipment for printing. Previously they hired it out; now they do their own. Literally tons of paper are used annually in the promotion of local church programs. Once you attend the church, you are on their mailing list *forever.* They feel that all you have to do is show an interest in them; they never know when some piece of literature will bring you back to make your decision for Christ.

They consistently buy the largest ad in the newspaper. They govern the size of their ad by the size of the other ads. If every other church is going five inches, they go seven inches. They have chosen always to have the largest ad so that no one will miss it.

Education. Thomas Road Baptist Church sponsors its own academy, Bible institute, college, and seminary. The purpose of all of these institutions is to train Christians to aggressively share their faith. Falwell has repeatedly said that his educational intention is to train young men who will build "superaggressive local churches," and that means evangelism within the walls. Interestingly enough, they write their own Sunday school literature so that evangelism will predominate.

TRANSFERABLE CONCEPTS

Aggressive leadership. Any church, regardless of its size, location, or tradition will flourish better with enthusiastic, involved leaders. At Thomas Road Baptist Church the pastor sets the pace. This is the usual pattern because churches ultimately become a lengthened shadow of the pastor's vision. Some churches, however, have come alive through the enthusiastic leadership of its laymen. You, as a lay person, could inspire your pastor and fellow members if you caught a vision for evangelism. Let God set your heart aflame. It is contagious. No church, anywhere, can overcome a lack of vision on the part of its leadership if it intends to move out for God.

Promotion. It is false piety to shun quality advertising. Exposure of the church and its message through the yellow pages, telephone contacts, billboards, local newspapers, radio, and television is consistent with our gospel mandate to "Go into all the world . . ." While a fear of Madison Avenue "polish" is valid, an avoidance of thoughtful promotional work is hardly defensible. If the world is lost, then we need to advertise the existence of people and programs geared to fulfilling the Great Commission. Your community should know that you exist and that you really care about its spiritual needs. Make your ministry known.

Without the Walls

Coral Ridge Presbyterian Church
Fort Lauderdale, Florida

COMMUNITY

Fort Lauderdale is a growing city of 165,000 population. In the past decade (1960-70) it increased at the rate of 67 percent; growth continues in the present decade at the rate of 40 percent. Some industry is located in the thirty square miles of the city, providing numerous blue-collar jobs, but white-collar workers continue to predominate the work force.

The balmy Florida climate (mean temperature in January

is 67.8; in July, 81.8) makes an apt location for tourists (well over two hundred motels and hotels) and a place for the elderly to retire. One out of five inhabitants is sixty-five years of age or over, and only one out of four inhabitants is under eighteen. A look at other communities included in this study underscores the "mature" nature of Fort Lauderdale. The median age of Palo Alto, California, is thirty-two; twenty-seven in Fullerton, California, and only twenty-five in Garden Grove, California. By contrast, the median age of Fort Lauderdale is thirty-nine.

The average income of the city places it in the middle income bracket for the nation as a whole although the residents of Fort Lauderdale (both white and black) average somewhat more than their counterparts in other Florida communities.

Fort Lauderdale has 198 churches of which there are fourteen Roman Catholic, forty-eight Baptist, and sixteen Presbyterian. This averages out to one church for every 833 persons.

In summary, Fort Lauderdale is a growing, medium-sized, white-collar, middle-income city with a sizeable retirement-age population. It is well churched.

CHURCH

The fastest growing congregation in the Presbyterian Church in the United States denomination began in 1961. Dr. James Kennedy, its dynamic senior minister, was its first pastor. In the last fourteen years, the Coral Ridge Presbyterian church has grown from nothing to over four thousand members (with peak attendance of over sixty-five hundred), from one minister to seven, and has recently completed a new church facility estimated to be worth approximately nine million dollars.

Kennedy was a dancing instructor with the Arthur Murray Dancing School and was rising quickly to prominence in his profession when early one morning his clock radio brought a disturbing question from Dr. Donald Grey Barnhouse, the famous Philadelphia preacher. It was the question regarding where he would spend eternity. The implication of that query resulted in Kennedy's revolutionary conversion.

Following graduation from the University of Tampa (B.A.), and Columbia Theological Seminary (B.D., cum laude), Kennedy went to Fort Lauderdale. The first year was a disaster. Instead of growing, the church declined. It was not until a fellow pastor taught him the secret of personal evangelism that the church began to move ahead. In the last few years, Kennedy has found time both to lead a church in a period of fantastic growth and to complete a Master of Theology degree from the Chicago Graduate School of Theology and a Ph.D. degree from the University of London.

Billy Graham, who uses Kennedy as a regular teacher in the Crusade School of Evangelism, cites two reasons for the phenomenal growth of this Fort Lauderdale church:

> The first is the unwavering devotion of Dr. Kennedy, as a man, to Jesus Christ his Lord, a devotion that counts no sacrifice too great, no cost too high to pay to give Jesus Christ his best. The second is the fact that Pastor Kennedy has recaptured the biblical concept that the Church's primary task is every-member evangelism. The Church, having come to Christ, is to go for Christ.

If you were to attend the Coral Ridge Presbyterian Church on a typical Sunday morning, you would neither hear an evangelistic message nor witness an altar call. Sunday services are devoted to worship and instruction. The relatively formal services include a choral introit, a recitation of the Apostles' Creed, the singing of the Gloria Patri, and classical anthems beautifully sung by the sanctuary choir. Sermons are generally expository in nature and doctrinal in content. A thoughtful, conservative theology is communicated week after week.

Evangelism is conducted in homes during the week, *not* in the church facilities during worship services, Sunday school ("School of Christian Living"), or at weekday activities.

PROGRAM

Over three hundred people are engaged in a weekly program of lay evangelism through the Coral Ridge Presbyterian Church. Five basic principles enunciated in Kennedy's book *Evangelism Explosion* undergird the endeavor:

1. "The Church is a body under orders by Christ to share the Gospel with the whole world."

   Thus it is that the church moves into the community to take the total initiative. Prospects include people who have visited a worship service (generally considered "the easiest people with whom to deal"), parents of children who attend Sunday school, the listing of those who have bought new homes in the area, and lastly, a house-to-house religious survey and opinion poll.

2. "Laymen as well as ministers must be trained to evangelize."

   The training is thorough and logical. Step-by-step the individual is taught a presentation of the Gospel. It begins with an introduction, which includes finding a point of reference in the home—hobbies, trophies, plaques, and so on—and discussing it; a word about the Coral Ridge Church; a word of personal testimony, and then the asking of two crucial questions:

(1) Have you come to a place in your spiritual life where you know for certain that if you were to die today you would go to heaven?

(2) Suppose that you were to die tonight and stand before God and he were to say to you, "Why should I let you into my heaven?" What would you say?

The next step is a presentation of the Gospel. This revolves around the grace of God, man's sinfulness, God's mercy and justice, the work of Christ, and the nature of faith. Each point is documented with Scripture. Finally, the visitors move to a point of commitment. This includes: the qualifying question ("Does this make sense?"); the commitment question ("Do you want to receive the gift of eternal life?"); the clarification of commitment; the prayer of commitment; and the assurance of salvation.

3. "Ministers must see themselves not as the star performer or virtuoso but rather as the coach of a well-trained and well-coordinated team." While the entire church staff works toward this goal, Archie B. Parrish, the minister of evangelism, focuses entirely upon this task of equipping laymen for their ministry.

4. "Evangelism is more caught than taught." Following a time of classroom instruction, groups of three go out on Wednesday mornings and Thursday evenings. Two of the three individuals are trainees. They receive on-the-job training by observing the trainer share Jesus Christ in the homes.

5. "It is more important to train a soul-winner than to win a soul." People are trained to evangelize by observing as others are being evangelized. The goal is for the trainees to become so proficient at evangelism that they can begin to train others.

TRANSFERABLE CONCEPTS

Go where the people are. Many of our neighbors do not know Christ. We need to take the initiative, find a point of contact, and lovingly present the gospel to them in their homes. For many of them, church attendance is not part of their life-style. They do, however, have needs that concerned, listening Christians can address, if they are given a hearing. The secret is found in mobilizing God's people for action. It only takes one person to begin the process. Prospects are already available in the vicinity of your church.

Equip for ministry. The Kennedy program is so complete that any Christian can read the training manual, memorize basic material, practice with friends, find a fellow Christian or two who will join him, and move out in faith, believing, to tell neighbors of Christ. Hundreds of churches and thousands of Christians testify to the joy that comes when one takes these steps of faith. In most situations a person, mature in faith, must carefully instruct trainees. The best instruction will include actual participation in home evangelism.

FOR ADDITIONAL READING

Falwell, Jerry, and Towns, Elmer. *Church Aflame.* Nashville, Tenn.: Impact Books, 1971.

Kennedy, D. James. *Evangelism Explosion.* Wheaton, Ill.: Tyndale House Publishers, 1970.

3
The Classroom Church

3

The Classroom Church

A GROWING NUMBER of churches are adopting the stance of a teaching institution. Week after week these congregations assemble to enjoy the benefits of meaty biblical exposition. No longer content to experiment with "the options to preaching," they have chosen to concentrate on preaching and teaching the Bible. By their definition, the church is *not* primarily a soul-winning station, a forum for contemporary issues, or a showcase for music and/or drama; it is a school house for the training of Christians. One theologian identifies these churches as "lay seminaries."

Large crowds in Dallas, Texas (First Baptist, W. A. Criswell, pastor), Newport Beach, California (Mariner's Church, Joe Aldrich, pastor), Panorama City, California (Grace Community Church of the Valley, John MacArthur, pastor), Waukesha, Wisconsin (Elmbrook Church, Stuart Briscoe, pastor), Long Beach, California (First Brethren, David Hocking, pastor), Costa Mesa, California (Calvary Chapel, Chuck Smith, pastor) testify to the attractiveness of this model.

People are hungry for spiritual nourishment. Studies

reveal that church people, even with years of attendance in Sunday school and at worship, know very little about the Bible. Too frequently congregations have been lulled into sleepiness with form and ritual, devoid of clear biblical teaching. Liturgy has its place, but not as a substitute for exposition of Christian truth in propositional form. Some churches have tried everything but preaching to reach people—drama, musicales, films, seminars, multi-media experiences, and so on. The swing is now back to basics! When people are fed, they will come.

Contemporary society acts as an ally for the classroom church. A lack of confidence in politics, intensified through Watergate and the resignations of the vice-president (Agnew) and president (Nixon), economic insecurity (heightened by unemployment and inflation), and the energy crisis combine to create a spirit of negativism and defeat. In the midst of multiple letdowns in society, man is reaching for something he can trust. Classroom churches proclaim a clear, confident word in a bewildered, pessimistic age. Here is a place where the truth can be heard. An authoritative word has never been more appreciated, and it is being expounded in both traditional and experimental fashion.

Traditional

First Evangelical Free Church
Fullerton, California

COMMUNITY

Fullerton, incorporated in 1904, is located twenty miles southeast of Los Angeles and twenty-five miles east of the Seaport Terminal of Long Beach.

Like many other communities in Orange County, it was once noted for its produce—oranges, walnuts, vegetables, hay, and grain. Today it houses over 325 manufacturing plants, with Hughes Aircraft Company (air defense environmental systems) and Beckman Instruments (electronic instruments) being the two largest.

With an average temperature of 62.2, Fullerton encourages outdoor living. In addition to an olympic-sized public swimming pool and a municipal golf course, there are no less than twenty-five city parks.

Between 1950 and 1960 the population of Fullerton quadrupled. The growth in the 1960s was marked, but in the '70s it has leveled off and become stable. In 1974 the population was ninety-one thousand with little likelihood of much growth in the next decade.

Fullerton is a middle-class suburban community with a net effective buying income of $15,500 per household (1974). In addition to its public schools, it supports a four-year university, a Christian college, a college of optometry, and a college of law. Biola College and Talbot Seminary are located in the adjacent community of La Mirada. Thirty-seven churches serve the community, averaging out to about one church for every twenty-five hundred people. In comparison to the other cities in our study, this is a relatively unchurched community.

In summary, Fullerton is a stable, middle-class suburban community with a predominantly white, though somewhat unchurched, population.

CHURCH

The First Evangelical Free Church of Fullerton was begun in September, 1955, as a daughter of the First

Evangelical Free Church of Los Angeles. The mother church invested ten thousand dollars and key laymen in the new work. A small 30' x 60' building, purchased from the Mormons on the location of the present facilities, served as the initial house of worship.

The first pastor, Wesley Gustafson, served faithfully for thirteen years. When he left in June, 1969, the church was in a very stable condition. The spirit was warm, the music was excellent, finances were sufficient, and attendance was around one thousand on Sunday mornings.

The search for a new pastor took more time than anyone would have imagined. Dr. Wallace Norling, the district superintendent, stepped in to serve as interim pastor for twenty-six months. He led the congregation in harmonious fashion until Charles R. Swindoll assumed the pastorate in late summer of 1971.

Swindoll, who was raised in Texas, served a tour of duty in the U.S. Marine Corps, eighteen months of which were spent in the Orient. During this time he felt called into the ministry of the gospel. Following four years of training, he graduated magna cum laude from Dallas Theological Seminary and was concurrently named recipient of three awards—one for outstanding achievement in the department of his major; another, the H. A. Ironside Award for expository preaching; and the third, the Faculty Award for the most outstanding graduate in the opinion of the faculty.

First Evangelical Free of Fullerton is Swindoll's fourth church. He previously served three relatively short pastorates in Dallas, Texas, Irving, Texas, and Waltham, Massachusetts. In Fullerton, God has blessed him as never before. The church is alive!

If you do not come early, it is almost impossible to find a place in the 956-seat auditorium on any given Sunday morning or evening. Attendance on Sunday morning averages around twenty-eight hundred; on Sunday evening it is fifteen hundred. It was necessary in September, 1975, to move to three morning services (8:15, 9:30, and 11:00) and two evening services (5:30 and 7:15). Prior to that time, three overflow rooms were required to accommodate the large crowds. Church membership, though never stressed, continues to climb. At present over fourteen hundred are listed on the active rolls. The church is now in the process of purchasing a twelve-and-one-half acre site on the corner of Brea and Bastanchury in Fullerton. A much-needed new facility is on the drawing board.

Much of the large mushrooming growth of the Fullerton Church is due to the effective pulpit ministry of Swindoll. People do not mind coming early and walking two blocks, due to woefully inadequate church parking, because they know that their pastor is well prepared and will give them a thoughtful exposition of Scripture. He is in the pulpit Sunday morning, Sunday evening, and at the midweek service on Wednesday night. A spirit of expectancy characterizes the church. It has become accustomed to a solid biblical menu.

PROGRAM

The weekly program at the First Evangelical Free Church is geared to the entire family. Sunday school classes, youth groups, women's groups, prayer groups, children's clubs, and choirs exist to minister to the variety of needs resident in the growing congregation.

For our purposes, however, concentration will center on that phase of the work that has been most instrumental in making the church grow, namely, the pulpit. The following distinguishing marks help define its uniqueness:

Sermons are expository. Instead of drawing his major points from an isolated text (textual preaching) or from a theme which determines the content of a message (topical preaching), Swindoll regularly chooses larger passages of Scripture for his sermonic consideration. Generally he uses a theme to tie the section (paragraph, chapter, or even more) together so that there is a cohesiveness to the study. Consideration is regularly given to the context of the passage, significant words with their past and present value, and the theological import of the section being studied. Interesting illustrations and anecdotes, interspersed throughout, are frequently homey and often humorous. Swindoll makes certain that just about every major idea is supported by presentday parallels, illustrations, and/or applications. The result is sermons that are biblical, pertinent, and interesting.

Sermons are longer than average. While the tendency in some churches is to shorten the sermon, the opposite is true at Fullerton. There seems to be a concurrence with the venerable Southern preacher Robert G. Lee who intoned that "sermonettes are preached by preacherettes and they produce Christianettes." Although Swindoll, like most classroom church pastors, preaches anywhere from forty-five minutes to an hour, no one seems to complain. From all indications, there is appreciation for this pattern, not criticism. It just may be that the length of the sermon is mandatory if the preacher is to do justice to an extended portion of the Bible.

Sermonic aids are provided. Upon entering the sanctuary you are provided a sheet of paper which lists the subject and text, introduces the theme of the day, and then outlines the sermon. Space is appropriately provided for the congregation to fill in additional material shared by the pastor during the course of his sermon. A healthy balance exists between providing information and leaving space for the layman to become involved. The reverse side of the sheet contains information entitled "Table Talk." This is provided so that families can read a verse or so of Scripture, discuss a theme, and pray together. Something is prepared for each day (Monday through Saturday) which is thematically related to the current sermon subject. In addition to these helpful aids, further reinforcements are found in printed sermons (provided a week or so after they are delivered) and in the extensive cassette ministry (weekly circulation has reached six hundred fifty). These sermonic aids help to clearly distinguish a "classroom church."

Laity expectations have undergone redefinition. The people of the First Evangelical Free Church do not expect their pastor to give much time to counseling, visiting, or administration. He is expected to be the teaching pastor. As such, he spends most of his time in the study. Other staff members counsel, visit, administrate, and direct the additional functions of the church. One layman bemoaned the fact that he could not be counseled by the senior pastor regarding a problem he faced, but he quickly added that he was extremely grateful for Swindoll's pulpit ministry and that it was worth the sacrifice. This choosing of priorities, by people and pastor, is necessary if the pulpit is to be vigorous.

TRANSFERABLE CONCEPTS

Interesting exposition is universally appreciated. The reason is shockingly clear—church people do not know their Bibles. Any pastor who is willing to pay the price to be a thoughtful expositor of Scripture will find grateful listeners. Dull preaching, even if it is true to the text, is a sin! But preaching which is anchored to the text, geared to the times, and full of human interest is always certain to have a hearing.

51

As one teacher of preaching once put it, "And now abides topical, textual, and expository; but the greatest of these is expository." Paul's advice to Timothy is still in order, "Preach the Word."

Good preaching is time-consuming. If you are a layman with a heart for God, you will do your best to free your pastor from jobs that can be assumed by laymen or other staff people. Ask yourself, Who can do the things that keep our pastor from spending time in his study? People are hungry for a clear word from God. This can only occur when the man God has called to this task is given prime time to prepare for that momentous assignment. Good biblical preaching takes large chunks of time!

Behavior is enforced through participation. Impression without expression is nil. That is why the thoughtful teacher/preacher uses every available form of reinforcement at his disposal. All that you need at the outset is some prior preparation and a duplicating machine. Learning will accelerate when aids are provided.

Experimental

Fellowship Bible Church
Dallas, Texas

COMMUNITY

Dallas was founded in 1841 by John Neely Bryan on the banks of the Trinity River. Located in north central Texas, in the rolling hills that form the upper limit of the Gulf Coastal Plain, it is approximately three hundred miles inland from the Gulf of Mexico.

Dallas, with a population of 940,000 (1974), is the eighth

largest city in the United States. The Dallas-Fort Worth area, with a population of 2,700,000, is the tenth largest metropolitan area in the United States. Both city and metropolitan area continue to grow.

The economy of Dallas is supported primarily by manufacturing, wholesale trade, and the petroleum industry. Over one hundred twenty petroleum-oriented firms, with a million dollars or more in assets, are headquartered in Dallas.

The Chamber of Commerce boasts that Dallas has the world's largest airport and that it is one of three American cities with the cleanest air. The average yearly temperature is 66.2. Fall, winter, and spring are comfortable, but the summers are frequently hot and humid.

The population of Dallas includes approximately 16 percent blacks, 6 percent Spanish, and less than 1 percent of all other nationality groups (Indian, Japanese, Chinese, Filipino, and so on).

According to the classified section of the phone directory (which is not exhaustive), Dallas has 1,140 churches and synagogues divided among approximately fifty-seven denominations. This averages out to one church for every 825 persons.

In summary, Dallas is a large city, well churched with all the usual heterogeneity that characterizes large American metropolitan centers. The community of North Dallas in which Fellowship Bible Church is located is more homogeneous. It is a middle- and upper-middle-class community with a predominantly white population.

CHURCH

Fellowship Bible Church met for the first time in a public meeting on Sunday, November 12, 1972. It was an auspicious start. One hundred thirty-nine persons gathered that day in the former Episcopalian church that had been rented with an option to purchase.

It all began when Dr. Gene Getz, associate professor of practical theology at Dallas Theological Seminary, and a nucleus of about twelve couples, schooled in traditional Bible-preaching churches, began to hunger for real, beneath-the-surface fellowship. They had known that kind of experience at retreats, but they wondered if it were possible to have the same fellowship in a local church.

Getz, an eager student all his life, combed the Scriptures to discover eternal principles which would give direction. Shortly thereafter, he and a small nucleus of concerned friends decided to start a new congregation in the midst of the already heavily populated Dallas church scene. Fellowship Bible Church was the place where the principles articulated by Getz in *Sharpening the Focus of the Church* were to be tested and tried. The experiment, from all indications, has been a success.

Dr. Gene Getz, a gifted high-school musician and basketball player from Indiana, sensed God's call to the ministry during high school. He moved to Chicago to earnestly study Christian education at Moody Bible Institute. Additional studies took him to Rocky Mountain College (B.A.), Wheaton College (M.A.), and New York University (Ph.D. in Christian Education). Prior to assuming leadership of the Dallas church, he taught Christian education at Moody Bible Institute and Dallas Theological Seminary (where he still teaches one course a semester).

To accommodate its growing numbers, Fellowship Bible Church sports four congregations: (1) Friday night (7:00-9:30), (2) Sunday morning (9:00-11:30), (3) Sunday afternoon (2:30-5:00), and (4) Sunday night (6:00-8:30). Each of the four services is identical in format. Well over a thousand people meet each week in this fresh environment of study and fellowship.

PROGRAM

Fellowship Bible Church is committed to a balance between instruction, fellowship, and witnessing. Acts 2:42-47 outlines the normative pattern for the church: (1) vital learning experiences with the Word of God (v. 42), (2) vital relational experiences with God and other believers (vv. 42, 45, 47), and (3) vital witnessing experiences with the unsaved world (v. 47). Getz asserts that an emphasis on any one or even two of those three norms for church life creates an unhealthy, carnal congregation. A mature church will discover a balance of all three.

My inclusion, therefore, of Fellowship Bible Church in the "classroom" category is partially suspect. Any church that places such a heavy emphasis upon fellowship, for example, ought also to be included in the life-situation classification.

In another sense it could be called a general practitioner church because it attempts to perform at least three functions (soul-winning, classroom, and life-situation). I include it in the "classroom" category because it manifests certain attributes of that form even though it also stresses the other needed emphases. Though a departure from typical teaching churches, it does incorporate the best of that form. Fellowship Bible is a teaching church, but it is much more.

There are two focuses of ministry—within the walls (for instruction and fellowship) and without the walls (ministering to your family, to your fellow Christians, and to your non-Christian friends).

The Gathered Church (Sunday A.M., P.M., or Friday P.M.).
Fellowship Bible Church features a two-pronged, two and one-half hour service for adults. The first hour Getz teaches a lesson from the Bible. He does this while sitting casually on a stool with an open Bible in hand and speaking in a conversational tone. The congregation is provided a printed guide to assist them during the message. The format typically includes: (1) an outline of the passage being studied; (2) a twentieth-century application; and (3) life response (a personal project for the week). This is spelled out specifically for three groups—families, children, and singles.

At the conclusion of this hour guests are acknowledged, and members of the congregation volunteer to serve as their personal hosts for the upcoming thirty-minute coffee break. Permanent name tags provided for regulars and temporary name tags for visitors assist people as they mingle together.

During the final hour, believers share their lives with each other. Some share a need, others a blessing. If a need surfaces, believers pray and often initiate the answer. Older children who were in their own classes during the first hour, join the adults for the sharing service. It is all quite relaxed. Children are sprawled on oversized pillows in the front of the sanctuary. If someone wants to share a song, he does so—at the piano or on a guitar; or someone may request a congregational song. Encouragement is given for believers to share their lives with one another.

A variety of good things have occurred at the second hour—believers have seen God work through his people to provide jobs, meet financial needs, begin to heal broken marriages, and satisfy a myriad of spiritual hungers.

During the adult two-and-one-half-hour session the children meet in the learning center. Every possible attempt is made to gear the experience with children to the thrust of

Getz's lesson with adults. Weekly sessions of teachers are for the purposes of coordination.

The Dispersed Church (in the homes). The minichurch concept is important at Fellowship Bible Church. Whenever twelve to fifteen new people come into the church they are formed into a minichurch led by a lay pastor-teacher, called an elder.

These minichurches meet a minimum of once a month for communion; most meet more often for prayer, Bible study, and sharing. Each week the elder calls his minichurch members (ten to twenty couples) to check on their spiritual progress and to learn of their prayer needs.

Being an elder at Fellowship Bible Church is more than meeting once a month to discuss church business. It involves weekly training from Getz and a commitment to ministry. Each elder is a pastor-teacher for his minichurch. He is to visit, encourage, counsel, and teach the members of his group. Membership as an elder is open to anyone who thinks he qualifies according to the scriptural standards (see *The Measure of a Man* by Getz).

TRANSFERABLE CONCEPTS

Christians are hungry for in-depth fellowship. If God's people are to share their lives in anything more than a superficial way, an environment must be created. While sharing is not for everybody, it does meet a need for many. Opportunities should be provided, but they must not be mandatory for everyone.

Concentrated learning is preferable to communication over-kill. In most of our churches there is biblical smorgasbord with the Sunday school, morning service, evening service, and midweek service each communicating a separate truth. As a result, some Christians do nothing because they do not know where to begin. The beauty of one teaching lesson a week is that it gives the congregation a distinct, unchallenged goal to pursue. It may be well for our churches to consider coordinating all the services of any given week so that they focus attention on a single biblical concept or challenge. We have too often overcommunicated and underapplied the gospel.

All God's people are ministers. The ordination of laymen as elders at Fellowship Bible Church helps to draw attention to the fallacy of assuming that only seminary-trained pastors are in the ministry. If you are a Christian, you are a minister. This fact is abundantly clear from Ephesians 4:1-16. Discover *your* gift and use it!

FOR ADDITIONAL READING

Getz, Gene A. *Sharpening the Focus of the Church*. Chicago: Moody Press, 1974.

_____. *The Measure of a Man*. Glendale, Cal.: Regal Books Division, G/L Publications, 1974.

Oliver, Kay. "Fellowship Plus!" *Moody Monthly*.

The Life-situation Church 4

4

The Life-Situation Church

MANY CONTEMPORARY CHURCHES are attempting to minister to the day-in, day-out concerns of John Q. Public. The response has been enthusiastic. Folks are encouraged to believe that in an age of hyperdepersonalization there are really people who care about them and their eight-to-five day. Rather than discussing abstract theological issues, life-situationists address persistent, earthy, human needs. This is comforting news for many!

The common denominator in life-situation churches is the importance of the individual. He is a person of great worth—created in the image of God, the very one for whom Christ died. He is loved and respected, unconditionally.

Bruce Larson, in *No Longer Strangers*, writes about this contemporary movement away from a systematic theology in the direction of a relational or visceral theology. The former appeals to man's reason and logic; the latter appeals to his feelings and emotions. While a recounting of theological nuggets still has great appeal for the academically oriented, there are throngs of people who would rather have someone feel with them and speak to their anxieties, hurts, and needs. This is the thrust of the life-situationists.

The spirit of this movement is found in Faith at Work conferences, Festivals of Hope, and the Serendipity sessions. Articulate leaders include Bruce Larson, Keith Miller, Lyman Coleman, Lloyd Ogilvie, and Norman Vincent Peale.

In an age of pessimism and despair when even Christians are wringing their hands, some churches are announcing hope. They declare that God loves you, you have great potential, we love you, and you *can* find fulfillment in the Christian experience. Life-situation churches are successful because they proclaim a message of hope in the midst of a troubled, confused, and hopeless age.

Two dissimilar churches serve as models—the Garden Grove Community Church, with its life-situation pulpit, and the Peninsula Bible Church with its life-situation "body life" services.

Garden Grove Community Church
Garden Grove, California

COMMUNITY

Garden Grove is centrally located in Orange County, the fastest growing major metropolitan area in California. The county is nestled between the Santa Ana mountains to the east and southeast, the Pacific Ocean to the west, and the large industrial complex of Los Angeles to the north.

Growth in Garden Grove was most rapid in the 1950s. While the county continues to grow at a faster rate than the rest of the state, the rapid expansion of recent years is being replaced by a slower, steadier rate of growth characteristic of maturing regions. Garden Grove, with a population of

123,000, has stabilized, and little additional growth is anticipated.

The median family income projected for Orange County in 1975 is $16,156. While Garden Grove is below average in Orange County ($15,051), it is above average for the state ($14,200). Trade, manufacturing, and government lead the way for the economy of the city.

There are seventy churches in Garden Grove. This averages out to about one church for every 1,750 persons.

In summary, Garden Grove is a stable, middle-income community with the typical suburban blend of commercial and residential. It is somewhat adequately churched.

CHURCH

The Garden Grove Community Church met for the first time at the Orange Drive-In Theater on March 27, 1955. When Robert Harold Schuller mounted the tar-paper-covered roof of the refreshment shop that day to proclaim the gospel, he saw only about seventy-five persons in fifty-one cars (forty in the audience were a "borrowed" choir from a neighboring church). It was a small beginning for the graduate of Hope College and Western Theological Seminary, but he was undaunted.

Through the "possibility thinking" of Schuller, the church, affiliated with the Reformed Church of America, has evolved into a congregation with 7,100 members and a multi-million dollar plant on a "twenty-two-acre shopping center for Jesus Christ." The current annual budget of 1.5 million dollars includes support of seventy-eight full-time persons, eight of whom are ordained ministers.

The burgeoning television outreach "Hour of Power" is carried on sixty stations coast to coast and is viewed weekly by two and one-half million persons. This Sunday morning telecast enjoys the highest rating of any religious program in four major cities—Chicago, New York, Philadelphia, and Washington, D.C. Each week the "Hour of Power" staff processes twenty thousand letters addressed to Schuller. The program, which operates on a budget of four million dollars, is self-supporting.

A beautiful 252-foot Tower of Hope dominates the church grounds. This fourteen-story building, topped by a ninety-two-foot neon-lighted cross, houses a twenty-four-hour telephone counseling service in the chapel at the top, offices for the growing staff, a counseling clinic, and classrooms for Christian education.

On Sunday morning there are three services (8:30, 10:00, and 11:15). In addition to the sanctuary, which is comfortably filled with seventeen hundred persons, there are hundreds of drive-in worshipers. From their cars, these people can watch Schuller (whose pulpit is open to the outside) and listen to the service by dialing their radio to the prescribed frequency. Because of continued growth, the congregation is currently raising ten million dollars to build a sanctuary which will seat four thousand and seven hundred persons.

C. Peter Wagner, the noted church growth theorist, states in Schuller's book *Your Church Has Real Possibilities* that any church which has a growth rate of 50 percent per decade is healthy and that 100 percent per decade is excellent. By contrast, Garden Grove Community Church grew at the rate of 505 percent from 1962 to 1972. They average seven hundred new members annually!

Schuller, inspired by Dr. Ray Lindquist (former pastor of First Presbyterian Church, Hollywood, California) who said that you should never take a church "unless you can envision spending your life there," and challenged by the record of

George Truett who spent forty years building the great First Baptist Church of Dallas, Texas, intends to spend his entire life of ministry in Garden Grove. That, he maintains, is the only way to dream big dreams and see them fulfilled.

PROGRAM

Many facets of the Garden Grove Community Church ministry could profitably bear investigation, not the least of which is L.M.T.C. (Lay Minister's Training Center). The faculty, drawn from all across Southern California, is enlisted to train one thousand lay persons. The goal is to have each person complete 224 units, the equivalent in hours to a seminary education. There are four principal areas of study: Bible, Christian life, church, and ministry. It is envisioned that laymen will be personally enriched in their Christian life, assisted to discover their gifts and abilities, and be trained in effective methods for Christian service.

For the purpose of this study, the temptation to pursue any additional ministries of this multifaceted church must be resisted. Attention should rather be focused on the "life-situation" pulpit of Schuller and in so doing review the successful ingredients which have facilitated growth in the Garden Grove Community Church.

Discover people's needs. This is hard work. The first year his church met in the rented drive-in theater, Schuller punched three thousand neighborhood doorbells seeking potential parishioners. He took careful note of the responses he received to his visits. When he discovered that folks did not attend any church, he told them he was delighted to hear this because he was anxious to find out how he could improve his church so that intelligent and wonderful people like them would want to come. He then proceeded to ask two questions: (1) Could you tell me what our church could possibly do to help in any area of your life? and (2) Is there any program that you would be interested in? During the last twenty years Schuller has responded to these and other articulated needs.

Although he is a competent Bible student as well as an authority on John Calvin's theology, he is most concerned to answer questions that outsiders raise. Schuller frequently asks fellow Christians, "Who are you trying to impress?" For Schuller, the answer is clear—the unchurched, the non-Christian. He wants to make his impression on the non-religious American, not the Christians or the "social workers in the county welfare department." Outsiders are impressed by many things—sincerity, success, beauty, modernity, and honesty, but most of all, by a church that answers *their* questions. It is essential, therefore, that these problems, questions, and needs be identified.

Preach on popular themes. Once the needs are understood, Schuller speaks directly to their solution. In his own words, "My job is to attract nonchurched people into the sanctuary on Sunday mornings through sermons that do not sound like sermons but which sound like helpful and inspiring messages." This problem-centered approach is one answer to Schuller's own slogan, "Find a need and fill it; find a hurt and heal it."

Schuller says that his job as senior minister is "to deliver messages that will bring great crowds to church on Sunday morning." What kind of sermons will do that? Read over the following list of representative sermon titles, and you will see a distinct pattern emerge. His sermons are contemporary, down-to-earth, and life-situational in character.

How to Get People to Treat You Beautifully!
How to Get Great People to Sincerely Admire You!

How to Turn Your Worst Time into Your Best Time!
How to Win Your World around You!
How to Satisfy Your Heart's Restless Passion!
How to Have a Life-changing Experience with God!

There is nothing archaic, stuffy, or abstract about any of them. Schuller patterns himself after Norman Vincent Peale, who also preaches on popular themes, the understanding of which requires little knowledge of the Bible or Christan thought patterns. Most of Schuller's public ministry revolves around the psychological needs of people. He is building a church which puts "strong wings on weary hearts."

TRANSFERABLE CONCEPTS.

Research your community to identify its needs. If you are genuinely willing to seek advice and counsel from your community, you will begin to identify some direction for an enlarged ministry. Meet the needs of your community, and it will beat a path to your door. While it is far easier to guess at community needs while comfortably seated with a committee in the church parlor, it is also far less accurate than if you were to go door to door. If you want the unchurched and non-Christians to visit your church, you must take the initiative to discover what will bring them to you. Be bold enough to inquire. It will be a valuable revelation upon which you can build a growing church.

Allow the Bible to meet human needs. Every Bible study, Sunday school lesson, and sermon should have as its goal the intersection of God's eternal truth and some clearly defined contemporary situation. Biblical truth without application to where people live is irrelevancy; whereas a study of contemporary need without the clear direction of the Bible lacks authority. As concerned Christians, we should endeavor to be both biblical and life-situational. A compromise of either dimension will weaken our usefulness in the kingdom of God.

Peninsula Bible Church
Palo Alto, California

COMMUNITY

Palo Alto dates back to the accidental discovery of the area by Spanish explorers. Don Gaspar de Portola and his men found the area during a frustrating search for Monterey during November of 1769. A redwood tree "El Palo Alto" (the tall stick) was the place where they camped. The city was not formally established, however, until 1889.

In the first three decades, Palo Alto grew slowly as a rural community. Today, it is a modest city of 53,000 that strikes a balance between industrial and commercial development and a quiet, tree-shaded residential community. Population growth was greatest between 1950 and 1960 when Palo Alto grew from 25,000 to 52,000. In the last fifteen years it has stabilized, and no additional growth is expected.

A buying income per household of $17,592 in 1973 placed it significantly above the average for the state. Homes in the city range in price from $35,000 to $200,000. In addition, the city average is only 2.4 persons per household.

Education plays a dominant role in the community. Two area community colleges have a cumulative enrollment of over 22,000 and much-respected Stanford University has an enrollment of approximately 12,500. Fifty churches, representing all major denominations, serve the community. This averages out to one church for every 1,060 persons.

In summary, Palo Alto is a stable, upper-middle-class

community with a predominantly white, educated, and adequately churched population.

CHURCH

Peninsula Bible Church or PBC, as it is known familiarly to its members, began in 1948 with just five businessmen who felt the need for a greater witness and fellowship than they had previously experienced. At first they met on Sunday nights in the Palo Alto Community Center, while still attending their own churches in the morning. A warm spirit pervaded the group, and it began to attract outsiders. At length they started a morning service. By the fall of 1950, their congregation numbered one hundred, and they felt it was time to call a pastor. Ray C. Stedman came in 1950 as their first full-time pastor. Much has transpired in the quarter-century since that union of people and pastor.

Stedman, a graduate of Whitworth College (B.A.) and Dallas Theological Seminary (Th.M.) has become a well-known figure in Christian circles. He is a popular speaker on campuses, at conferences, and in churches around the world. Most noteworthy of his gifts is that of teaching. His expositions of Scripture reach thousands through his pulpit, a printed ministry (Discovery Papers), and his writings (particularly *Body Life*).

The morning service at PBC is distinctly in the "classroom church" tradition. This service focuses upon the teaching ministry of the Word. Everything else is of bare-bones simplicity. A couple of hymns, the offering (when people are encouraged to visit with their neighbors), perhaps a solo (there is no choir), then the highlight of the morning—an expository sermon. Pastor Stedman, with open Bible in hand

and lavalier intact, carefully expounds a passage of Scripture for about forty minutes. The exposition is generally marked by clarity and logical and ample illustrations. Both services on Sunday morning are packed out. At the same time on Sunday morning, another ministry of the Word is conducted on the Stanford campus for up to four hundred students.

Sunday night at PBC is "body-life". This service qualifies the church for a life-situation classification. Here the conventionalities of Sunday morning are dismissed, and freedom is the rule. A standing-room only crowd of near a thousand shares and sings in the Spirit.

PROGRAM

The "body-life" service at PBC began in January, 1970, when the pastoral staff became concerned about the sparse attendance on Sunday nights. The conventional service drew 150-250, and only a few youth attended. After a time of soul-searching, they instituted "body-life" so that Christians could fulfill the function of edifying one another in love.

A few distinctive elements of "body-life" should be noted:

Informality. Everything about the service contributes to this mood, even the architecture. PBC has a plain, unadorned sanctuary shaped in the form of a cross. At a time when other churches of comparable size, influence, and financial ability are involved in multimillion-dollar building projects, PBC has chosen to stay in its simple facility. Aesthetics are not considered. The low platform area, the seating, the walls, and the ceiling are bland by contrast to the monuments to an architect's reputation that distinguish so many evangelical church facilities. No one is awed at PBC; it is simple and plain. Informality is part of the environment.

The tieless leader perched on a stool at the front sets the

tone for a folksy experience. Most of the audience is dressed
in casual attire. It seems that only a few, most probably the
visitors, are formally dressed. It is a comfortable feeling.

Spontaneity is encouraged. Testimonies, prayer, songs, or
the reading of Scripture do not follow an order of service.
Everything seems to unfold informally, but with decorum.
The evening blends the vertical dimension of worship and the
horizontal dimension of fellowship in a wholesome balance.

Importance of the individual. A major portion of the evening is devoted to sharing. The leader introduces the testimony
time, "We're the body of Christ, the family of God. He has
given us a variety of spiritual gifts. Let us share what God has
been doing with our gifts. Let us minister to one another."
Immediately hands go up all over the auditorium. A young
man with a cordless mike moves deftly through the crowd to
enable everyone to be heard.

A young man, with shining shoulder-length hair,
describes his sex trips and drug trips as "strictly nowhere."
Then he adds, "Last week I made the Jesus trip—or I guess I
should say that he found me—and, man, what love! I can't
get over it. I'm just a new Christian, but, man, this is where
it's at!" The delighted congregation claps and smiles as the
leader says, "Welcome to the family. What's your name?"

A divorcee with small children tells of unsolicited food
that came to her home when all she had was forty-two cents
to eat on that week. Everyone had eaten well, and she wanted
to express gratitude. Once again, the body applauds
enthusiastically.

A young, sensitive lady stands to tell of her brother who is
blowing his mind on LSD. The leader asks Phil, a tall, thin
youth with a scraggly beard, to stand by her and pray for this
urgent need. The whole audience bows as he prays with simple earnestness, "Oh, Father . . . Show him the way out,

through Jesus, and show him that you love him just the way he is."

A clean-cut college boy opens his Bible and shares a freshly discovered truth from 1 John. Everyone laughs with him as he makes an interesting though humorous practical application.

Needs continue to be shared. A student asks prayer regarding the ability to buy a car cheaply so that he won't have to depend on hitchhiking to get to his college classes on time. When the prayer is finished, a middle-aged housewife stands in the back and says, "I don't know how this happened, but just this week the Lord gave me a car I don't need. If Ernie wants it, here are the keys." The crowd applauds joyously as the blond boy runs to pick up the keys.

And so it goes. Sorrows are shared, and prayer is offered. Joys are shared, and everyone rejoices. The intensity of the experience is difficult to capture in words. It must be felt to be understood. One thing is certain—you and your needs are important!

Youthfulness. Seventy-five percent of the audience is under twenty-five years of age. The rest are young at heart. People of all ages are welcome and do attend, but the spirit of the meeting is best fitted to those who have the openness of today's student population. Formal, private people are likely to squirm while other types feel free to share in a Christianity marked by honesty, candor, and deep feelings.

TRANSFERABLE CONCEPTS

Christians need one another. Christians, whether in Palo Alto, California, or Dalbo, Minnesota, need the encouragement and strength which only fellow believers can provide. Joseph Parker said that "there is a broken heart in every pew," and he was absolutely right. Everyone has a burden to carry. The load is lighter when it is supported by two sets of shoulders.

While the "body-life" service functions best in an academic community where high premium is placed on verbal communication, the concept of caring is universally applicable. Sharing in love is not confined to formal gatherings. What is important is that people are sensitized to the needs of fellow Christians and are enabled to respond in healing, redemptive ways. The application of this truth will differ from community to community.

Christianity is a now faith. The local church can easily fall into the trap of sharing "disquisitions on ancient history" without struggling to show the nowness of Christianity. The message of the Bible is that the gospel is for people in the present tense. God is committed to the totality of our experiences—eating, working, playing, laughing, crying, loving, even sleeping. All of life is sacred. The "body-life" service underscores this relevance of faith to the commonplace. Any church that takes this seriously will find faith awakening in the lives of people who formerly dismissed it as an impertinence. Jesus is for now! Growing churches have learned that truth.

For Additional Reading

Schuller, Robert H. *Your Church Has Real Possibilities.* Glendale, Cal.: Regal Books Division. G/L Publications, 1974.

Stedman, Ray C. *Body Life.* Glendale, Cal.: Regal Books Division, G/L Publications, 1972.

The
Social
Action
Church

5

The Social Action Church

IN THE YEARS since the conclusion of World War II, a substantial number of churches have caught a vision for ministry in the community. Not content simply to work with their own membership, they have ventured courageously into the world to address emergent social needs.

It is generally understood that churches from mainline denominations, the Methodists, Presbyterians, and Episcopalians, have been at the forefront of this movement. This is only a partial truth. One thing is certain—there is no clear correlation between social involvement and theological liberalism. In the past, conservatives have been the leaders in social action (read Timothy L. Smith, *Revivalism and Social Reform in Mid-Nineteenth-Century America*). Today, as well, churches notable for their conservative theology are also playing important prophetic roles in society.

Socially conscious churches have arisen because Christians have a fresh appreciation for such basic texts as the Olivet Discourse (particularly Matthew 25, in which are recorded Christ's talks about feeding the hungry, providing a drink for the thirsty, clothing the naked, visiting the sick, and going to see the imprisoned); the Good Samaritan parable (which teaches that anyone in need is "my neighbor"), and the entire Book of James (which links true faith with tangible works in the home and community). In addition, many have come to view Jesus as a model for ministry. Did he not show obvious concern for the outcasts (Mary Magdalene, the woman of Samaria, and Zacchaeus), the sick (the lepers, the crippled, the blind), and the hungry (expressed dramatically in the feedings of the four thousand and the five thousand)?

Social action churches appeal to Christians whose conscience has been pricked by social injustice. They have properly maintained that when Jesus called us "to love our neighbor as ourself" it meant everyone—regardless of race, social standing, or religious commitment. A broken world issues the call to which social action churches respond.

Two dissimilar churches have been selected as models for this church type—the Church of the Saviour, Washington, D.C., which is thirty years old, small in size, stable in membership, but well known on the American church scene, and the College Church of Northampton, Massachusetts, which is young, rather large, growing in membership, but relatively unknown among American churchmen.

The Church of the Saviour
Washington, D.C.

COMMUNITY

Metro Washington, comprising the District of Columbia and ten adjacent communities, is situated between the Blue Ridge Mountains on the west and the Chesapeake Bay on the east. It straddles the Potomac River, one of the nation's best-known and historic waterways.

This community is distinctive for many reasons: (1) it is the political center of the United States; (2) it is the fastest-growing large metropolitan area in the nation; (3) it entertains approximately twenty million visitors each year; and (4) unemployment rates are significantly lower than for the nation as a whole. In January, 1972, for example, Metro Washington unemployment was at 2.3 percent, while the national unemployment rate was almost three times as large.

Metro Washington is the best educated metropolitan area in the nation. One in every four adults in the eleven communities is a college graduate—a proportion that is almost twice as high as the average of the twenty-nine other leading metropolitan areas.

The area boasts an income per household that is 30 percent above the national average. However, Washington, D.C., treated as a separate entity, matches the national average. It is the poorest of the eleven communities that comprise the metropolitan area.

Washington, D.C., is predominantly a nonwhite community of 720,000 population. Approximately 75 percent of the metropolitan area is white, while almost 75 percent of the capitol city is black. The surrounding counties and cities have had an exploding population during the past decade, but Washington, D.C., has remained stable. There are approximately 550 churches in Washington, averaging out to one church for every 1300 persons. Many of these, however, appear to be of the "storefront" variety.

In summary, Washington, D.C., is a unique city providing offices for some of the most powerful political figures in the world. It is a middle-class, predominantly black community, surrounded by a highly educated, upper-middle-class, predominantly white metropolitan area of ten cities, each of which is smaller than the capitol city.

CHURCH

The first official meeting of the Church of the Saviour took place on a Saturday afternoon, October 5, 1946, at the First Baptist Church, Alexandria, Virginia. According to its constitution, it was to be a church "with a distinctive ecumenical spirit and approach, allowing freedom of worship, practice, and belief among its own constituents, while remaining true to the basic values in the stream of historic evangelical Christianty." Gordon Cosby, the only pastor the church has ever known, wanted to build a church where people were committed to Christ and to one another, where religious divisions were healed, and where the mission was to take a world for Christ. Three decades later those goals are still intact.

On October 22, 1950, a twenty-five-room Victorian mansion located at 2025 Massachusetts Avenue and purchased for $60,000 was dedicated as the Church of the Saviour, an ecumenical church. That brownstone house has served since then as headquarters for the church. It houses a chapel, classrooms, library, offices, dining room, and reception hall.

In the attempt to bring integrity to its membership, rigorous standards were established. The School of Christian Living offered six courses—Old Testament, New Testament, Doctrine, Christian Growth, Ethics, and Stewardship—which prospective church members were required to take. Each course was twelve weeks in length, used textbooks, and concluded with exams. Upon the successful completion of all courses and the recommendation of a sponsor (who had worked with the candidate for a few weeks or even months), the individual joined the church on the basis of a covenant to read the Bible and pray daily, worship weekly, be a vital contributing member of one of the mission groups, and give proportionately, beginning at a tithe. This commitment was to be remade annually in the month of October. Each year when a few could not recommit, they were dropped from the active membership roll.

Each of the churches included in this book has enjoyed significant growth in membership and attendance. With some, the growth rate has been staggering; with the Church of the Saviour it has been slow. Emphasis has been placed upon the qualitative, not the quantitative. As a result of this emphasis, expressed in the demanding membership requirements, the congregation in 1968, twenty-two years after its inception, numbered only 250. This church, by its very nature, never will have an impressive array of statistics.

PROGRAM

Through its history, the church has attempted to keep the "inward journey" (the life of devotion, expressed through worship, small prayer groups, and study programs) and the "outward journey" (the life of service in society) in a creative tension. Members are convinced that one journey is shallow and lacks substance without the other. Reconciliation takes place in the heart as well as in the world.

A basic premise of the Church of the Saviour states that "there is no Christian community not rooted in service." This service takes many forms, all of which are based on the premise that each person is called to minister, and because gifts and interest of individuals differ, so will their ministries. The mission groups of the church give definition to ministry; through them the Church of the Saviour finds its shape.

Mission groups are in a constant state of flux. New ones

are occasionally added, and old ones are sometimes modified or even dropped. Just three of the mission groups will be considered.

THE POTTER'S HOUSE

About 1960, the church opened its storefront coffee house, where six nights a week the church could meet the world. Shoppers, artists, poets, moviegoers, businessmen, politicians, and scientists come to enjoy the art work, sip coffee, and exchange conversation in a congenial environment.

This places a heavy responsibility on the seventy members of the coffee house mission group, each of whom is expected to give one night (usually 7:00 P.M. to 1:00 A.M.) each week. There are only three paid positions: coffeemaker, dishwasher, and cleaning help. Members volunteer for all other tasks, such as cashier, administrator, waitress, or host.

Three words define the purpose of the coffee-house ministry—presence, service, and dialogue.

Presence. Although personal evangelism in its well-recognized form does not flourish within its walls, Elizabeth O'Connor says that the members are there to say "the wise thing at the appropriate moment." Members act themselves. "God is the evangelist" and "the Spirit is at work."

Service. Using Jesus as their model when he took a basin and washed the feet of his friends, the Church of the Saviour insists that the people of God need to recover their servant role. This has not been easy.

Gordon Cosby tells of the time he gave three addresses at a large American university. For the days that he was there, everyone called him Doctor. He corrected this several times, but they persisted in giving him the title. Immediately after this experience he returned to Washington, D.C., in time to serve and "bus" tables at the Potter's House. It was a busy and hectic night. He was hurrying to clear a table when a customer snapped his fingers and said in a surly tone, "Hey, boy!" "There arose in me," said Gordon, "the feeling, 'Don't you know who I am? I don't have to do this.' " Servanthood has not been an easy lesson for anyone to learn.

Dialogue. An atmosphere of openness encourages visitors to share freely. Here with members with who have learned the importance of listening, they discover friends who will "weep when they weep" and "rejoice when they rejoice." Very frequently, hostile, alienated, lonely persons find clues to a Christian solution.

THE RESTORATION CORPS

The story of this mission group is the story of a half-dozen people who discovered a mission in the midst of an unmet need in Washington, D.C. One person in particular, Sharon Avery, went from mission group to mission group, but found none of them personally satisfying. She was miserable—at home, at work, and at church. It was not until she put her interior decorating gift to work that she found her place.

She and a handful of others became serious about a mission to the inner city, a ministry that would see them painting and repairing broken-down slum tenements so that the families living in them could stay together. When one building was completed, they would move on to repair another. On occasion, the group would purchase the buildings and then repair them.

The work was often hard—trash to be moved, furniture to

be hauled, floors to be scraped, and walls to be painted. It was dirty, smelly work which often ended with people yelling at each other. They were learning things about themselves, even as they were serving others.

After Restoration Corps was authorized as a mission of the church, it was incorporated under the laws of the District of Columbia as the Community Restoration Corps.

FLOC (FOR LOVE OF CHILDREN)

For years the newspapers had run feature articles and editorials on the plight of the inhabitants of Junior Village, the district's dismal institution for homeless children. The place was overcrowded and understaffed. At length, a group at the Church of the Saviour decided to do something about the decaying situation.

Letters were sent to fifteen hundred churches in the Washington area to enlist their support. It was envisioned that if just one hundred of these churches would each form a mission group to be personally responsible for finding homes for ten children, Junior Village would close down. Although one hundred pastors came to the briefing session, only a handful were willing to make a commitment. An ecumenical council was formed and the work began.

FLOC moved along slowly, finally shifting its emphasis from a crusade to small committed and disciplined mission groups. Not only were children placed in foster homes, but homes were purchased or rented for Junior Village families, rent subsidies were provided as needed, and each reunited family was provided supporting friendships.

Eighteen months after the formation of FLOC the population of Junior Village was down from 910 to 560. Progress had been made. A spirit of hope was present.

TRANSFERABLE CONCEPTS

The Christian life is both devotion and service. Maturing Christians are discovering that a life of devotion, worship, and learning without service is an irrelevancy. Paul says, "We are . . . created in Christ Jesus for good works, which God prepared beforehand, that we should walk in them" (Eph. 2:10, RSV). On the other hand, service that does not spring from a heart warmed by the presence of God is little better than arid humanism. The proper rhythm for God's people is "in" for worship (corporate and personal) and "out" for service.

Gifts provide a clue for ministry. The church has a responsibility to define, uncover, and use the gifts resident in its membership. The ministry of the church should be shaped and redefined as it discovers what gifts are included among its people. The more common tactic adopted by churchmen is to have predetermined slots into which "ungifted," uninterested people are sometimes dropped. The Church of the Saviour bears witness to the wisdom of allowing its people to form groups which give expression to their particular gifts. If there are groups which match the membership's talents, this is fine. If not, new dimensions of ministry are necessary—places where people can give useful expression of God's gifting.

The College Church
Northampton, Massachusetts

COMMUNITY

Northampton, located in the Pioneer Valley of western Massachusetts, is a small city with a proud reputation. Here the Great Awakening under Jonathan Edwards (1703-58) began. The church he pastored still stands as a reminder of a movement which influenced an entire nation during the mid-eighteenth century.

Northampton, with its 35,000 inhabitants, represents the sociological spectrum. There is industry, farming (the second largest asparagus-producing center in America is here), and a bustling academic community. The city has a racial mix of whites, blacks, orientals, and Asians; the majority of non-whites are related to the academic community.

Northampton is in the center of what is commonly referred to as the Five-College Area. Three schools are in the small (10,000 population) adjacent town of Amherst—University of Massachusetts with 25,000 students, Amherst College with 2,000 male students, and little Hampshire College. The prestigious women's institution, Smith College, is located in Northampton (2,500 students), and Mount Holyoke, another well-known women's college, is in the neighboring town of South Hadley. The total student population of this small geographical section is in excess of thirty thousand.

Seventeen Protestant and six Roman Catholic churches serve the city. If half of Northampton is Roman Catholic as estimated by residents, then there is one church for every 1100 Protestants.

In summary, Northampton is an amply churched, relatively small, heterogeneous community, so influenced by education that it gears its business and social activities to parallel the academic year.

CHURCH

In October, 1970, Paul MacVittie began a seventeen-month interim pastorate of a denominational church in

Florence, a village of Northampton. During that extended period, contacts were made with the business, professional, and academic community which gave birth to the idea of starting an interdenominational community church.

On April 15, 1972, the first worship service of the College Church was held in the rented gymnasium-auditorium of the former Northampton School for Girls. Preparation for that first meeting was thorough—radio advertising, the newspaper media, prayer vigils, plus word-of-mouth enthusiasm generated by the initial group of ten members. Over three hundred people attended the first worship service.

MacVittie, a graduate of Gordon-Conwell Divinity School, served two New England churches prior to becoming founding pastor of the College Church. Under his leadership, the College Church has been progressive in methodology and relational in theology. The Apostles' Creed is cited by the church as an expression of its theological stance.

The property rented for the first service is now owned by the church. The seven acres of land, gymnasium-auditorium, and office space were valued at $1,000,000 and were acquired for $415,000. In addition, the church has free use of two state-owned buildings, located just across the street, which provide twenty extra classrooms in exchange for the use of the gymnasium one hour a day by mentally retarded teens.

Contrary to a popular church pattern which lists far more members on the roll than attendees, membership at the College Church is only 135 family units; attendance at Sunday morning worship averages close to 800; this is the highest average for any Protestant church in western Massachusetts.

Leadership is distributed among a staff of four full-time men (the pastor, an administrative assistant, an associate pastor, and a Christian education director), three part-time men, and three full-time secretaries. The current budget is $120,000, and indebtedness is less than $50,000.

Growth has been so steady month after month that it has been called the "fastest growing church in New England." Every effort has been made to balance this growth between biological growth, transfer growth, and conversion growth. In a recent three-month period, forty-eight new adults joined the membership, 50 percent of whom represented conversion growth. Long-term goals, enumerated by the pastor, include: (1) Institute for Christian Living, (2) membership of 1,500, (3) extension center for Fuller Theological Seminary, (4) creation of satellite churches, and (5) a private Christian academy.

PROGRAM

Some of the ministry at College Church is traditional— Sunday worship, Sunday school, a day-camp program, a preschool and kindergarten. Many churches had followed this pattern. However, basic to the vitality and growth of this particular church is a unique practice which places it in the social-action church category. It is the concept of "Total Mobilization." Everybody, according to this principle, has a task to do.

A twofold commitment is necessary to join the church, a commitment to Christ and a commitment to the community. This means that not only is the new member a Christian, but he is willing to use his time and talents for a ministry in the community. In order to facilitate this double commitment, an associate pastor was hired as a special ministry director. His job is to involve the people in a ministry for which God has gifted them. Rather than indiscriminately placing people in jobs, an attempt is made to discover what gifts they have and then to place each individual accordingly. This produces

Christians who are happy in their assignment, fulfilled because they sense they are making a vital contribution, and blessed by God with spiritual fruit. Because of this requirement for each one to have a specific ministry, the church is made up of nuclear members rather than fringe or token members.

When a new person joins the church, he meets with the elders, after which he signs a twofold commitment as he officially joins the membership. Then the associate pastor sets in action the process whereby the new member is enabled to identify his talents (which he has had since birth) and his gifts (which he received at the time of his New Birth). The next step is placement.

It is expected that every member will average at least two hours per week in some form of ministry with non-Christians. It is possible that he may do very little for two or three weeks and then work for eight hours in a single day. The key is regular involvement—for every member.

Every week hundreds of College Church people are serving Christ in the community. Large crews of volunteers work at the three Northampton hospitals—a state mental hospital, a VA hospital, and the Cooley Dickinson Hospital. Others serve in the five rest homes, providing visitation, services, and kindness. One man regularly takes someone from a convalescent home as his personal guest to football and basketball games. After a recent rain storm, two church members repaired the leaky roof of an elderly couple's home. The Drop-In Center, owned by the city, has many volunteers provided by the church. A federally supported program called Supplemental Security Income (SSI), which exists to complement Social Security funding for elderly people, received attention when thirty church members made literally thousands of calls to Northampton area retirees. They were

89

able to find over one hundred eligible people. The newspapers carried the story of this unusual congregation that really cares—in tangible ways—for its community. A weekly publication, mailed to the congregation, keeps everyone informed of new areas of need and opportunity. The associate pastor serves essentially as the placement director; he often puts people and tasks together.

A part-time staff member in his sixties works with the Golden Agers of the community. Each week he conducts tours to points of interest. After the tour, each guest is treated to refreshments and a brief devotional. The majority of people involved on a weekly basis are not members of College Church. It is just another way in which believers express love to their community. It is little wonder that the College Church continues to grow. It has developed a great reputation!

TRANSFERABLE CONCEPTS

Total mobilization. One hallmark of growing churches is the breadth of involvement among its members. The Communist Party knows the wisdom of this principle; every party member is a willing worker. Churches will grow and members will be personally fulfilled when "total mobilization" is a clearly defined goal. Congregations full of unused, untapped people carry an albatross around their neck, which could be fatal. All of God's people were saved to serve.

Identification with the community. A stance of aloofness by the local church has two detrimental effects—members lose an opportunity to minister, and the community dismisses the church as an irrelevancy. When a congregation takes its neighborhood seriously, it often discovers that the effect is reciprocal: the community takes the church seriously.

Church growth, however, is a by-product of identification. First and foremost is the mandate for Christians to love the unlovely, then show mercy to the needy, and to assist anyone when there is cause. The reciprocal benefits are a bonus. Believers are to minister without promise of benefit.

FOR ADDITIONAL READING

O'Connor, Elizabeth. *Call to Commitment.* New York: Harper & Row, Publishers, 1963.

_____. *Journey Inward, Journey Outward.* New York: Harper & Row, Publishers, 1968.

Smith, Timothy L. *Revivalism and Social Reform in Mid-Nineteenth-Century America.* New York: Abingdon Press, 1957.

6

The General Practitioner Church

6

The General Practitioner Church

THE CHURCH OF JESUS CHRIST is a potent force in our world. In every corner of the globe there is a witness to the redemptive power of the Savior. Local congregations are being used in our day as never before. What a great time to be alive! With all the effective work going on, why can't *we* plug into some of that life? We can! Churches everywhere are finding clues from others, clues which have strengthened their local usefulness.

In previous chapters we have reviewed four models of success. In each instance God is blessing in phenomenal ways. No two works are alike. We are forced to confess that there is no single sacrosanct pattern. One type is evangelistic—the lost are finding Christ. That is good. Another type majors on teaching—Christians are growing. That is good. A third type is addressing pressing personal needs—Christians are finding help for their daily lives. That is good. A fourth type is meeting the social needs of its community—these Christians are the salt of the earth. That is good. It is all very good!

Paul in his letter to the Colossians says that we are to proclaim Christ "warning every man and teaching every man in all wisdom, that we may present every man mature in Christ" (Col. 1:28, RSV). Our message is Christ, and our goal is maturity. In other words, the purpose of the church is to make men whole. This means whole toward God (evangelism), whole toward truth (doctrine and teaching), whole toward life (life-situational), and whole toward society (prophetic). It is my personal conviction that all four emphases need to be stressed in the typical local church. Obviously this is a huge task. It may be more effective to major in one and minor in the others. However, every community has all four needs. Should not the church reflect this?

The present chapter is an autobiographical account of just one congregation, the Whittier Area Baptist Fellowship, that is committed to learning from all four types. We do not have all the answers; so we need help. Fortunately, the questions we ask have been answered by others. We are trying to glean from them. The result is a general practitioner church. We are not specialists, to use the parlance of medicine; we are practicing family medicine. We thank God for every specialist church; we, however, have chosen a different route.

It is risky business to advertise your own church. The attempt is always fraught with problems:

Difficulty No. 1 is that you may think we are a model of success. The truth of the matter is that we often fail—sometimes miserably. Some months ago I taught a course in personal evangelism for over one hundred people. The attendees were enthusiastic, the material was logical and thorough, and I was elated. It was to be the start of a dynamic evangelistic outreach into our community. It all misfired. After the course was over, just about everyone went back to business as usual. It lacked something—leadership, follow-through, or something. All I know is that we flunked that test. Our story is sprinkled (or should I as a Baptist say "immersed"?) with failures. So cheer up. Maybe you can learn from our failures.

Difficulty No. 2 is that you may think I can do all four tasks equally well. On the contrary, like every other Christian in the world, God did not choose to bestow all the gifts of the Spirit on me. I wish he had. If only I had the gift of evangelism. It would be thrilling to see hundreds come to Christ through my evangelistic work. It is not true. Certainly I lead people to faith in the Savior, but there are laymen in our church who do it better than I do. Bless their hearts! I wish I had the gift of administration. It would be exciting to dream, plan, organize, and lead like Robert Schuller does. That is not me! Fortunately, God knows my weaknesses and surrounds me with people who have administrative gifts.

Difficulty No. 3 is that you may think we, and we only, have the truth. Far from it! We know there are thousands of churches who are attempting comparable exploits for God. Many do it better than we do. I tell our story, not because we are masters of success, but because I know it best. Bear with us as we flounder, but join us as we test, try, and even risk for the glory of God. We do not expect you to mimic us, but we hope that you will join us as learners in the school of the church. There is too much going on for us to be myopic. Open your eyes. God is alive. The church, his body in the world, is alive and doing well. Learn what you can.

Whittier Area Baptist Fellowship
Whittier, California

COMMUNITY

Whittier, hometown of the thirty-seventh president of the United States, Richard M. Nixon, was founded as a Quaker colony in 1887. These earliest residents emphasized tolerance, brotherly concern, temperance, and responsibility. They championed free enterprise, yet practiced the Quaker creed that no man should reach financially beyond his ability to manage. Upon such values, engraved deeply in the Whittier matrix, the city has grown to a stable population of 72,000.

Growth, like that of many Southern California communities, was dramatic in the period 1950-70 when it tripled from 23,000 to 72,000. No significant additional growth is anticipated in the future since most of the twelve square miles are now populated. There is, however, an increase in the percentage of Mexican-American residents.

Whittier is in the southeast corner of Los Angeles County, fifteen miles east of downtown Los Angeles on the southwestern slopes of the Puente Hills. It supports numerous public schools, Rio Hondo Community College, and Whittier College, a private institution.

In its earlier days, Whittier was known primarily as a residential community; more recently it is becoming a center for industry, warehousing, and corporation headquarters.

The population is distributed from the lower-middle-income to the upper-income brackets. Most of the population is within the middle-income range, but a growing number of more proserous residents now populate the northeastern corner of the city (Friendly Hills).

There are seventy-four churches representing at least thirty denominations in Whittier. Included are two synagogues, three large Roman Catholic churches, three Mormon wards, and twelve Baptist churches. There is approximately one church for every 970 residents.

In summary, Whittier is a stable, middle-class residential and industrial community, with a growing Mexican-American population. It is quite adequately churched.

CHURCH

The Whittier Area Baptist Fellowship (WABF) was born in the hearts of folks who wanted a ministry that was conservative in theology, loving in spirit, and flexible in form. A group of over three hundred drawn from a large Baptist church which was fast becoming autocratic and legalistic, held its first public meeting in a rented school on August 5, 1971. The atmosphere was electric. The services were well attended, joyful in Spirit, and love was in great evidence. Those early months, I have been told, were exciting indeed.

A gifted young man, now pastor in Ann Arbor, Michigan, came during the first month to serve as the sole full-time staff member. He wore many hats: administrator, Christian education director, visitor, counselor, and worship leader. Guest preachers filled the pulpit Sunday after Sunday.

February, 1972, WABF moved into the rented facilities which we still share with the East Whittier United Methodist Church. They needed the additional revenue; we needed a new home. It has been a most congenial relationship. The Methodists meet for Sunday school and worship at 9:30 A.M.; the Baptists worship at 11:00 A.M. and conduct Sunday school at 5:45 P.M. The sole evening service is conducted by WABF at 7:00 P.M.

In the spring of 1972, WABF was formally received into the Baptist General Conference, a denomination of 700 churches, 118,000 members, and a well-known reputation for warm, progressive evangelicalism.

When I came as pastor on the first Sunday of August, 1972, it signaled a dramatic change in my life. For the previous eight years (1964-72) I had taught preaching, pastoral leadership, and related subjects at Bethel Theological Seminary in St. Paul, Minnesota. Although I had nine interim pastorates during those years, that was far different from being a full-time pastor. The transition from classroom to parish ministry was greatly abetted by the presence of numerous able laymen and a competent staff.

People have been patient, and God has been good. We have grown steadily to a membership of 850. Attendance is around 800 in the morning and 450 in the evening. In 1972 we received total monies of $137,000. The figure for 1974 was $354,000.

Under the influence of Robert Schuller who stresses visibility and accessibility, a committee began the search for our own church property. Everything that was visible and accessible was too expensive (as much as $100,000 an acre.) Finally, by the marvelous grace of God, we were enabled to purchase twenty-two acres of the choicest land in the whole area—for only $10,000 an acre. Five of the acres, which adjoin the Friendly Hills Country Club eleventh fairway, were sold to a developer for the construction of quality homes. Our architect has drawn a master plan for the development of the seventeen acres of rolling land which fronts on Colima Avenue, with its twenty-four-thousand-cars-a-day exposure. Our location is a link between Whittier and the fast-growing area of Hacienda Heights and Rowland Heights. The first phase, projected for completion in August, 1976, will include a parking lot for four hundred cars and a large, attractive building with a lower level for Christian education space and an upper level for offices, small kitchen, and a combination fellowship hall-sanctuary which will seat one thousand worshipers in fifteen rows of wrap-around seating.

One outstanding evidence of the commitment of the congregation is the fact that they purchased in excess of $1,000,000 in church debentures during the summer of 1975 to help underwrite the building project. This, incidentally, at a time when money was tight and everyone was cautioned to be conservative. A quality program needs quality leadership. We believe we have that kind of people.

Our staff includes two full-time pastors, two secretaries, and four half-time workers—a preschool coordinator, a children's coordinator, a junior-high/niner coordinator, and a high school/college coordinator. Other paid staff include an experimental worship leader, a small group leader, an associate music director, a worship leader, and two organists. An excellent choir director volunteers his service, as does our competent adult coordinator.

Inasmuch as there are three hundred thousand unchurched individuals living within fifteen minutes' driving distance of our corner, we believe the goal of tripling in the next decade is challenging, but reasonable. The opportunity is great.

PROGRAM

Earlier I noted that the WABF is a general practitioner church. We attempt to incorporate all four emphases—soul-winning, classroom, life-situation, and social action—into our ministry. Let me explain how this works out in practice:

EVANGELISM (soul-winning model)

The biblical message is clear. All men are sinners (Rom. 3:10, 23; 6:23) and need a Savior. Jesus Christ died for our salvation (Rom. 5:9). We become Christians by responding to the grace of God in an act of personal repentance and faith (John 3:16; Rom. 10:9, 10; Eph. 2:8, 9). Our purpose as a church must include the announcement of this Good News. We do this in three ways:

Pulpit ministry. We regularly include an evangelistic sermon at one of our Sunday services. Most often it is in the morning. As we preach through a biblical book (recent series have included Psalms, Ephesians, and Galatians) or a series (recent topics: apostles, life of Christ, and gifts of the Holy Spirit), we allow the text to speak its evangelistic message. Whenever the text is evangelistic, I give an invitation for people to respond (altar call, raised hands, see us at the door, or write in on a card). On one occasion, I gave an altar call even though the message was not evangelistic when I felt particularly led of the Holy Spirit to do so. It was thrilling to see ten people come forward. This, however, is an infrequent practice. Invitations tend to be as frequent as the passage from which the sermon is taken is evangelistic.

Week-night visitation. A study of evangelistic methods convinced us that the program of James Kennedy outlined in *Evangelism Explosion* was adaptable to our church. Each week we have teams of two or three individuals who go out to share Christ in homes. The regular night is Monday although some have called on Wednesday nights and during the day on Saturday. While the results have not been dramatic, they have been encouraging.

A few folks, with a particular heart for evangelism, go out every week. God is blessing the church through them. We believe that this area of ministry has great potential for the future. We want to see people trusting Christ regularly. We must work harder at enlistment of workers for this cause.

Encouragement for evangelism. In addition to classes on personal evangelism taught in our Sunday school, we invite testimonies at our Wednesday or Sunday night services which highlight evangelism. We have been encouraged recently by teachers who win their students, employers who win employees, students who win classmates, and a variety of others who win friends and neighbors. This is particularly gratifying because the ministry belongs to all God's people. The staff exists to train and equip our "eight hundred ministers."

We encourage evangelism as often as we can. This means that we do it in sermons, Sunday school lessons, at camps and retreats, in counseling, and through the provision of free printed materials for the congregation. Each week we refill a rack that is stocked with *The Four Spiritual Laws* booklet. This publication of Campus Crusade has been an effective tool for many as they share Christ.

TEACHING (classroom model)

Our congregation, like every other congregation in the world, needs further training in the truths of Christianity. There is just no known substitute for thoughtful, accurate, and interesting biblical exposition. The goal is for people to know what they believe (2 Tim. 2:15) so that they may know the truth, live by the truth, and ultimately share the truth with others (2 Tim. 2:2).

The classroom motif exists at three points in our program:

Christian education. Traditionally, our Sunday school has been dedicated to a study of God's Word. Our emphasis is no different. The one variation from some other church programs is the availability of elective classes reaching down into the high school area. Many churches provide electives for adults. On occasion we do the same. We believe that high-school students should also be given the opportunity to choose the area of study that matches their needs and their understanding of the Christian faith.

In addition to Sunday study, we have an extended Bible study for adults on Wednesday. In the last three years we have primarily studied Mark, Romans, and the doctrine of grace. This study is verse by verse with ample opportunity for interaction, discussion, and questions. Concurrent studies are provided for high schoolers and another for collegians. One of our men has ably conducted a Bible study for laymen during the past year. A number of our ladies also meet in groups to study the Word and pray together.

Pulpit exposition. Almost every sermon deals with an extended portion of Scripture which is expounded in the light of its historic setting as well as in its relevance for today. I consciously distinguish three levels of truth: (1) *Past*—the historic, cultural, grammatical meaning of the text. That is, what did it mean to its original audience? We look at the context, the meaning of the words used, the culture to which it was addressed, and particularly to the meaning intended by the Holy Spirit who inspired it. (2) *Always*—what is the theology of the text? What truth about God informs that particular situation or setting? It is the theology of the text that gives it its reigning authority in every age (whether it be 700 B.C., A.D. 80, or 1976). This truth is always the same. In other words, parts of the Scripture, though inspired, are not normative for today (for example, the Levitical offerings). There is, however, in these time-bound situations something revealed about God which is *always* true. It is that truth which we need to underscore for the believer. All of Scripture is inspired of God and authoritative, though not always normative for the Christian in the twentieth century (additional examples: the holy kiss, footwashing, or the length of hair). (3) *Present*—no sermon is complete without application. Though I never know in advance how the Holy Spirit may choose to apply the truth of Scripture to any given individual, I consider it my responsibility to make suggestions, to illustrate possible applications, and to acknowledge parallels to today's scene. In the final analysis, only God can apply it to the individual. The pastor is, at best, a mediator of that process.

Special teaching series. During the last two years, I have had three special series that were distinctly in the classroom tradition. The first was a thirteen-week study of doctrine using the Apostles' Creed as the outline. The next was a five-week series on the cults. During this period we reviewed such groups as the Mormons and Jehovah's Witnesses. The most recent series extended over four months and was a sequential study of Paul's Letter to the Galatians. Each message was in the forty- to fifty-minute category and was supported by extensively developed printed materials to assist the learning process and to provide data for later reference.

LIFE-SITUATION

Either the gospel is significant for our life here and now or it is irrelevant. We must either begin in Jerusalem and end in Whittier or begin in Whittier and end in Jerusalem. It is both thus *said* the Lord and thus *saith* the Lord. The Christian life is present tense. Among the areas where some progress is discernible are the following:

Pulpit Every single sermon is an attempt to grapple with some current need of our people. It is necessary, therefore, for me to be in touch with the people. My goal is to spend equal time with books and with people (visitation, hospital calls, and counseling). Many of my colleagues in multiple-staff churches choose to relinquish pastoral person-centered ministries to associates. I jealously guard the pastoral dimension of ministry. I can all too quickly degenerate into idle chatter and irrelevancies unless there is regular in-depth involvement with the dear folks for whom the gospel is intended. Gladly will I surrender administrative chores, but preaching and pastoral work, for me, are two sides of the same coin. Life-situation preaching depends on contact with real people and their needs. Occasionally I have invited lay people into my office to help me prepare the sermon. These visits are invaluable for all of us.

Worship and Witness Service. Inasmuch as we can only meet at one hour on Sunday morning (11:00 A.M.), we very early in our life together at WABF had a problem. Our sanctuary could not hold everybody. One day an interested layman hit upon an idea that has been a Godsend. We now provide two separate and concurrent types of Sunday morning worship experience—a traditional service (hymns, Scripture, prayer, offering, special music, choir, and sermon) and a nontraditional service. Although we were forced into this format, we are now convinced that it was of God. For the informal service (called "Worship and Witness") we meet in the fellowship hall. Chairs are wrapped around a platform-worship center, and I sit on a stool to preach at the beginning of the service. When I leave at about 11:28 A.M. to go to the sanctuary for the traditional service, opportunity is given for congregational involvement. In addition to singing and the giving of an offering, there are two forms of expression intended to help the congregation apply the gospel to its life.

The first is an unstructured time called "Minister's Report." This gives those in attendance a brief time to publicly respond to the message of the morning. It is usually testimonial in nature. For example, "I never realized how easy it is to backslide. I confess that I have a heart of unbelief. Pray with me that I may be more obedient to my Lord." Or, "I met the Lord today. He knew I needed encouragement from his Word."

The second opportunity is carefully planned. Committee

members with one Sunday a month as their responsibility plan a response to the message. Our talented experimental worship leader works with these individuals. I sit in with him and the committee chairmen during an overall planning session to answer questions about proposed sermon themes and texts for the following three months. Examples:

Message	*Response*
"Growing Old Gracefully"	Interviews with four people about seventy years of age
"Forgiveness"	Congregation shared how they felt when forgiven. ("red balloon," "sand through toes," "wind through hair," "weight fell off my shoulders.")
"Ethics"	Three short dramatic scenes depicted situations where a Christian had to decide (honesty, liquor, etc.).
"Christmas Message"	A multimedia presentation
"Priorities"	Each person present wrote out a list of five specific items where he intended to do something.
"Witnessing"	Two short skits—first: how not to witness; second: a better way to witness

Circles of Concern. The congregation is broken down into twenty-five circles which meet on a regular basis. Membership is voluntary; no one is forced to participate. Each circle averages about seven families who meet monthly for a study night. One month they gather in the twenty-five homes for Bible study, discussion, sharing, and prayer; the next month at church for a meeting of adults only. These sessions occur on Wednesday. A social night (such as potluck dinner, game night, beach party, attending a baseball game, attending a play, out to a restaurant for breakfast, even week-end camp-

107

ing) is conducted by each circle every month. The nature of the socials is determined by the individual circles. Groupings change each year to encourage people to make new friends and to cut down the likelihood of cliques (which, let's face it, happen regardless of how you scheme, plan, or pray).

Circle leaders are chosen because of their commitment to a caring ministry. It is the responsibility of these individuals to pray for each member of their circle at least once a week, to lead the studies and socials, to keep in regular contact with all members (phone them if absent for awhile; encourage their participation in WABF life), visit sick and delinquent members, and communicate emergent needs to the pastoral staff.

Circles have become small churches within the larger church. They provide places where individuals are known, loved, and cared for on a much more personal basis. They enable our people to "weep with those who weep" and "rejoice with those who rejoice." A member of WABF, trained in both theology and psychology, is Circle of Concern coordinator. He helps us integrate two worlds—the biblical and the life-situational.

SOCIAL ACTION

This is the area where we do the least and struggle the most. We have, however, made some feeble attempts:

Projects. In 1974 we raised approximately four thousand dollars for World Relief through a program sponsored by World Vision. We put plaster-of-Paris "love loaves" on our tables to remind us of those in need. It was common for our people to put coins in the loaves during every meal. It was an exciting day when hundreds brought their "love loaves" to be broken, counted the money, and then deposited it in a plastic globe with a big hole in the top. It is our biggest endeavor to date for World Relief. Tokenism, to be sure, but a start in the right direction.

We have adopted a beautiful Vietnamese family of seven members. WABF, through the loving gifts of its members, is providing housing, necessary transportation, furniture, help with employment, and about five hundred dollars a month until the family can become self-sufficient.

At Christmas we adopted two sister churches—a black congregation in Pomona and an Indian congregation in South Gate. Our congregation bought gifts for these friends (names, items needed, and sizes were listed on two large sign-up sheets) and also provided money for whatever needs were current in the respective churches. Incidentally, the money in Pomona made up the necessary difference for the December rent bill.

The congregation recently gathered signatures on a petition calling for a referendum on a recent law in California, signed by the governor, which favors leniency on homosexuality. Although the drive failed to generate sufficient signatures statewide, it got our people involved in the political process.

Personal involvement. WABF encourages its members to be active in the community. This means, as a minimum, that every Christian should vote in every election. Romans 13:1-7 is instructive for us.

We have constituents at WABF who run for political office, who serve on the Whittier Planning Commission, and who work vitally in campaigns to elect officials who represent Christian convictions.

There is much more that we should do in the days ahead. We want to be known as a church that cares for the needs of its community.

TRANSFERABLE CONCEPTS

Be a gleaner. We unashamedly learn from anybody who can assist us. Evangelistic methods came from Coral Ridge Presbyterian Church; our classroom outlines were inspired by both Charles Swindoll and Gene Getz; our choice of church property was influenced by the perspective of Robert Schuller; and occasional "body-life" services in our fellowship hall on Sunday nights bear a resemblance to a service by the same name at Palo Alto. We thank God for these friends whose ministry has overflowed on our congregation.

Be an optimist. People choose one of two directions for their life—positive or negative. The former type is consistent with our view of future things as revealed in the Bible. If Christ is the Lord of history, then we are the people of an exciting destiny. Even when things are bleak, we know the one before "whom every knee shall bow." Negative people kill the work of God. They forget to whom they belong, why they are here, and what the gospel is all about. Optimism is a psychological term describing faith. Positive, affirmative churches have a contagion that every community needs. I believe that one of the most attractive features of WABF is its loving spirit and affirmative style of ministry. If you tend to be a "hand-wringing · sourpuss," let God redeem your emotions and your vision.

Provide options within your church. Part of our calling to faith includes a commitment to the eternal gospel. Some things never change—man's need (sin), God's love (universal), Christ's work (salvation provided). Structures, however, are not sacred. They are either helpful or they are not. It is unfortunate when God's people do not recognize the diversity of needs, temperaments, and tastes represented by their colleagues in the body of Christ. It is an established fact that some worship best in a formal, liturgical setting, while others need a more relazed, informal environment in which to have a meaningful encounter with their Lord! Both forms are legitimate.

Our two concurrent services on Sunday morning—one traditional, the other contemporary—is our own way of recognizing that no single format will be equally effective in reaching everyone. Be careful that your church does not freeze form; keep the gospel changeless and sturctures flexible!

Be as diversified as your community. Church growth, by definition, is often related to "homogeneous units." Peter Wagner's thesis is that growth occurs among groups that find a common ground or a narrowed focus of ministry. This, it appears to us, is subject to modification. We believe, that a new typology arises, namely, a university (separate colleges within the university may legitimately become "homogeneous units"). Work hard to make everyone (regardless of class, education, or race) who lives in your community feel at home in your church.

7
What's Next?

7

What's Next?

IT IS TIME to pause and reflect. How do you feel? What thoughts do you have? What emotions can you identify? Is it possible that you are enthusiastic about the possibilities of the church in general but feel rather frustrated with your own particular church? Take heart! That alternating set of emotions is normal. In fact, that very tension is an omen of better things. Without it there is no stimulation to change; with it comes the pressure to resolve the tension.

It should be clear by this time that the churches whose stories have been rehearsed, and the pastors who guide them, are unique. It follows, therefore, that it would be foolish to transplant programs indiscriminately. That is not the message of this book. However, before you decide to carry on "business as usual" in your church, remember these two things: (1) No program anywhere is sacred. Structures are either useful or they are not. (2) Principles alone are sacred. They transcend programs and localities.

Your task as a concerned churchman is to do the best possible job of fulfilling the Great Commission in your community. *Principles* of truth drawn from the particular situations reviewed in earlier chapters have been gleaned for *possible* implementation in your church. Very likely, the programs will differ. Each setting needs indigenous structures (programs tailored to that particular community). "Evangelism Explosion" program from Coral Ridge Presbyterian or the "body-life" service of Palo Alto, though fantastic in certain situations, may not work in your church. The principles behind these programs, however, should still be considered.

A PERSONAL WORD FOR LAY PEOPLE

As a Christian, you are a minister of the gospel. God has placed pastors and teachers in the church to equip you for ministry. Neither ordination nor formal theological training is necessary in order for you to perform that ministry. What you do need is a heart that is warm toward God and a personality that is yielded to the control of the Holy Spirit. Everything else is secondary. Consider, therefore, the following:

BE TEACHABLE

Keep your mind open to fresh truth. Closed minds freeze categories and, thus, rule out the Holy Spirit. While it is always traumatic to break away from comfortable patterns of church life, it may occasionally be necessary. It is essential to distinguish what is absolute (such as the nature of God, the deity of Christ, the sinfulness of man, redemption through Christ's death and resurrection, and so on) from what is nonabsolute (such as Sunday morning service at 11:00 A.M., midweek service on Wednesday night, an offering at every

116

Sunday service, and so on). Absolutes are to be cherished, but nonabsolutes are subject to prayerful, careful scrutiny.

A few Christians, noted for their low threshhold of boredom, enjoy change for its own sake. They are in constant flux, moving from one idea to another. This is a dangerous syndrome. Much church life, though distinctly in the nonabsolute category, deserves to be perpetuated. If the purposes of the gospel are being accomplished, it is unnecessary to change. All changes should arise out of a clear understanding of what God wants to accomplish through his church in the local church. If programs obstruct, deter, or confuse the mandate of the gospel, then they are suspect, but not until then.

A wise layman sees his walk with God as an adventure and himself as a dynamic, spirit-led adventurer. To be sure, there are risks when people become open to God, but that is the prerequisite of revival. Keep open to change in the nonabsolutes, while committed in love to that which is eternally established and true. In other words, be a learner; the Holy Spirit is in the teaching business.

AFFIRM PASTORAL LEADERSHIP

Pastors, in spite of the caricature to the contrary, are very human. They have days of great triumph when they ascend their Mount Carmels to call down fire on the enemies of God, but they also know the depression of the desert place. Ironically, this frequently follows immediately after a great victory. So it was with Elijah when he encountered Jezebel after the extraordinary victory on the mountain top.

Your pastor needs occasional encouragement. If he has been used of God in your life, tell him. He needs to know that he is useful and appreciated. It is not necessary to do this every week, but share it when you feel it. If you find it hard to express in person, drop him a note. Give credit and praise when they are deserved.

Why labor this? Satan uses discouragement, criticism, and even the silence of well-intended Christians to disable those in leadership capacities. Pastors, being human, rally to honest affirmation; they need the encouragement that you can offer. It can be part of their enablement for greater effectiveness. No church will grow with discouraged leadership.

DREAM DREAMS

You are involved in a team ministry with your pastor. Not only does this mean participation on committees and faithfulness to assigned tasks, but it means a shared vision.

No one knows in advance through whom God may choose to speak. It could be through you to an entire congregation. This can happen when you walk with God. As you read his Word and as you pray, ask God to bring times of refreshment to your church. He has been known to answer that prayer. In fact, he delights in responding to that brand of faith.

Churches used of God in extraordinary ways have the unmistakable input of vision brought by laymen who love Christ and his church. Dream dreams for the glory of God! Let some of the principles from effective, growing churches germinate in your heart.

A word of caution is now in order. Be sensitive as you share your vision with pastoral leadership. If you are not careful, your ideas will be treated as a criticism of existing programs which are ultimately viewed as an extension of your pastor. New ideas could sound like an attack on him. That is one very good reason why you should be affirming your pastor for the good work he does. New ideas against the backdrop of honest appreciation are more readily accepted. When you share your dreams, do so in a spirit of love and humility.

Remember, your dreams may be inspired by God, or they could be the result of indigestion. If they are of God, they merit a hearing.

BE FAITHFUL IN YOUR MINISTRY

If you are a Christian, then you are gifted. The Holy Spirit has sovereignly distributed gifts to every believer. This is abundantly clear from 1 Corinthians 12:7 and Ephesians 4:7. A study of the gifts of the Holy Spirit outlined in Romans 12:6 ff., 1 Corinthians 12:8-11, and Ephesians 4:11, 12 will reveal great diversity. The purpose of this gifting is for the benefit of the body of Christ (1 Cor. 12:7, Eph. 4:12 ff.). The challenge is twofold: (1) Know your gift(s) and (2) Use it (them) for the work of ministry.

In 1 Corinthians 4:2, Paul enunciates a basic standard for all Christians: "It is required of stewards that one be found trustworthy" (RSV). The word for trustworthy was used by the Greeks when they spoke of the confidence they had in their weapons. Paul was saying, in essence, that God expects his people to function well, to be reliable instruments in his hands.

The practical outworking of this principle means that you will volunteer to serve (consistent with your gifts), that you will prayerfully support the work of God with your time, talent, and treasure, and that you will view your role as strategic and complementary.

In summary, the world has yet to see what God can do through an army of laymen who are teachable, affirming, visionary, and faithful. God bless your ministry!

A PERSONAL WORD FOR PASTORS

Your position is one of magnificent potential. Pastors chart the course of the local church. It is threatening, but true, that your church will ultimately be an extension of your vision. It is of utmost urgency, therefore, that you consider the implications of this reality. What are you trying to do? How are you going about it? Are you happy? Discouraged? Excited? Depressed? If you are normal, you have tasted a little bit of each. Regardless of how you feel, the church does need you.

As a fellow traveler on the highway of the church, allow me to hazard some suggestions:

BE YOURSELF

One of life's greatest temptations is to emulate successful people. In part, this is fine. It may cause you to stretch. If, however, it creates a pathological dissatisfaction with yourself, then it is unfortunate. God's will for you is still to be you! However, be the best you possible; that is what faithfulness is all about.

The goal in church life is not to parrot Falwell's superaggressive leadership, Kennedy's superb neighborhood evangelism, Swindoll's teaching style, Getz's balance between instruction and fellowship, Schuller's possibility thinking, Stedman's "body-life" service, Cosby's penetration of the community, or MacVittie's twofold commitment. Rather, it is to learn what you can from each. Let the overarching principles take root in your soul. Maybe God will provide a vision, consistent with *your* personality, that you can implement. A superficial transporting of programs from someone else's church to yours is a hazardous practice which courts disaster for people and pastor alike. Ideas must soak through your personality and be thoroughly digested before they can be shared.

Some things are not for you. Do not feel guilty about that. Thank God for men and churches dissimilar from where you are; then move on to do the work God has uniquely equipped you to perform.

BUILD CREDIBILITY

Aristotle spoke of three ingredients in persuasion—*logos* (reason or rationality), *pathos* (emotion), and *ethos* (credibility). He insisted that ethos is the most important of the three. In his words, "We believe a good man." Contemporary research in behavioral change supports the thesis that a man's credibility is extremely important if he is to lead people in change.

When congregations attempt fresh exploits in a community, they need to be solidly behind their leaders. A man's credibility is the foundation upon which this can be built. Your people must have confidence in you as a person. They must believe that you merit their support.

How is credibility established? Everything you do—preaching, teaching, visiting, moderating a committee, socializing, even yard work—is part of the data fed into your ethos computer. Your trustworthiness, your knowledgability, and your dynamism combine to give you credibility. Your people perceive this in you. If they have come to trust you as preacher, you are likely to have their support when you rally them around new programs geared to church growth.

Young pastors and pastors fresh in a church need to build solidly. Let the people know of your love for Christ. Let them benefit from basic biblical exposition. Let them get close to your heart and sense your concern. At least a year of basic, stable ministry should precede significant change. The reasons are clear: (1) Your parishioners need to trust you before they will tolerate modification in their patterns of church life; (2) you need to know the questions before you dispense answers. Trained counselors know that direction is given only after the client has thoroughly rehearsed his need. Then, and then only, should answers be forthcoming.

This may sound intolerable. The church you serve may strike you as antiquated and irrelevant. As such, you may feel that it needs to be shocked immediately out of its lethargy. I feel with you, brother, but I beg time. Go too quickly, and it will boomerang in your face. The very people you want to change will become resistant. Rather than experiencing church growth, you may suffer through decline. Patience is difficult for all of us. We need, however, more of it if our ministry is to be crowned with blessing. Credibility takes time to establish. If your church needs to get moving, great. Be certain, however, that your people believe in your leadership as you move ahead.

BE POSITIVE

One of two orientations is available to you—that of the optimist or that of the pessimist. The optimist focuses upon the grace of God; the pessimist, upon the problems of man. Biblical Christians should have a theology of hope. Those, on the other hand, who fix their gaze on the world around them become prophets of doom and harbingers of bad tidings. This is not to suggest that you live an ethereal existence, divorced from the grubby realities of a sick world, but it is to suggest that a fixation on malady is not the way toward recovery of

Appendices

Appendix A
FIRST EVANGELICAL FREE CHURCH
Fullerton, California
Charles Swindoll, Pastor

DOING RIGHT WHEN YOU'VE BEEN DONE WRONG*

James 5:7-12

We have all experienced the hurt of mistreatment and misunderstanding. Such hurts come in a variety of packages: an intolerable working situation; domestic conflicts; a parent, child, or relative who takes advantage of us; a friend who turns against us; a neighbor who entertains untrue opinions of us; and dozens of other painful circumstances. Our natural tendency is to retaliate, to return evil for evil, to "get back," to hold a grudge and become bitter in our souls.

God has a better idea! James reveals this alternative in the passage we're considering this morning. He not only tells us *what* to do in place of retaliation, he tells us *how* to do it.

I. Introduction Problem

A. Our Natural Reaction

B. God's Supernatural Alternative

*Thirteenth message in the expository series on James. The fourteenth will be presented tonight from James 5:13-16 entitled "Suffering, Sickness, Sin—and Healing." A sequel will be presented on Wednesday: "Why Some are *Not* Healed."

II. Exposition Passage (James 5:7-12)

  A. General Observations

    1.

    2.

    3.

    4.

  B. Specific Explanation

    1.

    2.

    3.

    4.

III. Application Principle

January 5, 1975 (A.M.)

TABLE TALK

The following statements and questions are designed to pro-voke discussion and in-depth thought on the things we considered Sunday morning. Following one meal each day, push the dirty dishes back and consider these things for ten or fifteen minutes. Keep your Bible handy—and above all, be honest! A brief time of prayer is always a good way to end your "table talk."

Monday, January 6

Read 1 Peter 2:18-20 . . . slowly and thoughtfully. Give special attention to the situation being presented ("those who are unreasonable . . . those suffering unjustly"). Honestly talk over the difficulty of putting these verses into practice by sharing some ac-tual instances in your own life. Mediatate upon "this finds favor with God" in verse 20.

Tuesday, January 7

Go back to the Peter passage you looked at yesterday. Read it again along with verses 21 through 25. Why does Peter illustrate his point by referring to Christ? Pray for specific situations that resemble this need for patient submission in your life right now.

Wednesday, January 8

James 5:7 is the verse for today. It talks about *patience*. Are you? Why . . . or why not? Discuss the *implementation* of this verse. What are some of the techniques that have helped you overcome impatience? Share freely.

Thursday, January 9

Read James 5:8-9 aloud. Can you find the three commands? Go over each one with some thought. Especially camp on the one in verse 9, "Do not complain!" Are you a negative and critical person . . . a grumbler . . . a grudge-holder? Admit it openly and ask for prayer.

Friday, January 10

Read James 5:10-11 with a good deal of thought. Talk about either the life of an Old Testament prophet or Job's trial. Picture yourself in that situation. Consider the words "The *outcome* of the Lord's dealings" in light of Hebrews 12:11-13.

Saturday, January 11

By spending time in James 5:12, ask God for insight in the control of your tongue when caught in the squeeze of mistreatment and misunderstanding. Honestly discuss your "breaking point" and talk about how to overcome it.

Appendix B
FELLOWSHIP BIBLE CHURCH
Dallas, Texas
Gene A. Getz, Pastor

September 15, 1974

SERIES TITLE: MOSES—A MAN GOD USED!

A. Moses was a man God used.
B. Why was Moses so greatly used by God?
C. Why is Moses an outstanding example for study?

MOSES' PARENTS—AN EXAMPLE TO FOLLOW
(Exod. 1; 2:1-10)

Moses was conceived during a time of great stress for Israel. The prospect of his birth placed his parents in an extremely difficult position. The problem they faced was gigantic and awesome.

A. The Background of the Problem (Exod. 1:1-22)

1. Multiplication of Israel.
2. Mobilization against Israel.
   First, Pharaoh tried to demoralize Israel. Second, Pharaoh tried to kill all the newborn boy babies. Third, he ordered every newborn male to be cast into the Nile.

B. How Moses' Parents Faced the Problem (Exod. 1:1-10)

1. They had faith.
2. They had courage.
3. They had a strategy.

A TWENTIETH-CENTURY APPLICATION

What can a story like this—so far removed from our culture and experience—teach us today?

First of all, the early years of Moses' life had a great influence on his thinking and attitudes, even though he grew up in a pagan environment. Those first four or five years in his parents' home, before he went to live in the king's palace, marked him for life. He never was able to forget God and his own people.

The application is obvious. As parents—or future parents—do you realize how important your influence is in the early years of your child's life? It's not so much what you teach him didactically, but rather it is what *you are*—your actions, your attitudes, even your tone of voice! A child who observes parents who love God, who love each other, and who love their neighbors as themselves can never get away from that influence!

Second, a pagan culture—no matter how degenerate—need not destroy our children, but it will take the same factors in our lives as those in Moses' parents.

1. We, too, must have *faith* in God—faith that he will help us and help our children to become followers of Jesus Christ.

2. We, too, must have *courage*—boldness to stand against the tide of materialism, secularism, and sensualism that are bombarding our children every day.

3. We, too, must have *strategy*. Faith and courage are but the foundations upon which we must build. We'll never save our children from Satan's plot to destroy them by merely trusting God. We must act on our faith!

How do you measure up to these biblical criteria? Have you combined faith, courage, and a strategy to bring up your children "in the discipline and instruction of the Lord" (Eph. 6:4)?

The church and Christian schools can only assist. They can never do what the home has failed to do! They can only build upon a parental foundation.

Remember: It is never too late to begin, though it is more difficult when our children are older. What can you do to take the first step—right now?

LIFE RESPONSE

As a parent, I am going to take the following *first step* to better prepare my children to follow Jesus Christ:

FOLLOW-UP PROJECT

Family: As a husband and wife, compare notes with each other. What steps can you take together to develop a strategy to achieve the goal for effective family nurture?

Children: Cooperate with your parents, no matter what your age, as they attempt to follow through on this project. Remember the words of Paul: "Children obey your parents in the Lord, for this is right. Honor your father and mother (which is the First Commandment with a promise) that it may be well with you and that you will live long on the earth" (Eph. 6:2, 3).

Singles: Using the church directory, select one family from the church to pray for on a regular basis. Call the family and let them know you are praying for them as a result of this message. *Note:* If someone has already chosen a certain family, select another until you find one that has not been chosen. *Suggestion:* You might try to find a family that has the same initials as yours.

Appendix C
WHITTIER AREA BAPTIST FELLOWSHIP
Whittier, California
Dan Baumann, Pastor

GALATIANS
Let's Get It Straight—Salvation
Is by Faith
Galatians 2:11-21

I. Introduction

One of man's age-old questions is, How can I be right with God? Consciously or unconsciously most people assume that a good life (full of kind deeds, right motives, and proper behavior patterns) is the way to divine approval. The Bible takes issue with this teaching. Man can only be right with God through faith in Jesus Christ. Everything short of that commitment is inadequate.

II. Exposition
   A. Hypocrisy Condemned (vv. 11-14)
      1. Showdown with Peter (v. 11)
      2. Division at the Love Feast (v. 12).
      3. Influence of Peter (v. 13)
      4. Public rebuke of Peter (v. 14)
   B. Faith in Christ—My Only Hope (vv. 15-19)
      1. Justification by faith (vv. 15, 16)
         a. The futility of the law
         b. The universality of the provision
      2. Possible blasphemy (v. 17)
      3. The Law is dead (vv. 18, 19)
   C. Complete in Him (vv. 20, 21)
      1. The crucified life (v. 20)
      2. The grace of God (v. 21)

III. Application
   A. The body of Christ is one.
   B. We cannot earn the favor of God.
   C. Successful spiritual living requires daily dependence on Christ.

IV. Project for the Week
   A. Reread Galatians 2:11-21.
   B. If you have never surrendered your life in faith to Jesus Christ, do so. Your good works will not satisfy his perfect standards. Receive Christ as God's own provision for your life—now and eternally.
   C. Seek to correct any fractured relationships you have with fellow Christians. Take the initiative—prayerfully.
   D. Read Galatians 3:1-14 in preparation for our next study on "The Bewitching Time—Spiritual Relapse."

GALATIANS
The Bewitching Time—Spiritual Relapse
Galatians 3:1-14

I. Introduction
   Any Christian can backslide. It is for this reason that the Scripture warns, "Let him who thinks he stands take heed lest he fall" (1 Cor. 10:12). Backsliding takes different forms. For some it is carelessness regarding the things of God; for others it may be forgetfulness or callousness. For the Galatians, and some modern Christians as well, it is a matter of defection—moving from the truth to error. This substitution is always a step backwards. Christians must, therefore, be vigilant regarding their relationship with Jesus Christ.

II. Exposition
   We now begin the *doctrinal* section of Galatians (chaps. 3-4).

136

We have completed the *personal* section (chaps. 1-2), and we shall later consider the *practical* section (chaps. 5-6).

The True Gospel Explained:

A. The Argument from Experience (vv. 1-5)
 1. Bewitched (v. 1)
 2. Questions that demand an answer (vv. 2-5)
    a. How did you receive the Holy Spirit? (v. 2)
    b. On what basis are you maturing? (v. 3)
    c. Did you suffer in vain? (v. 4)
    d. What is the basis of divine miracles? (v. 5)
B. The Argument from Scripture (vv. 6-9)
 1. Abraham's faith (v. 6)
 2. Those who believe after Abraham (vv. 7-9)
C. The Argument from the Cross (vv. 1-14)
 1. The law demands perfection (vv.10, 11*a*)
 2. The just live by faith (v. 11*b*)
 3. Two distinct means of being right with God (v. 12)
 4. The curse and blessing of the cross (vv. 13, 14)

III. Application
 A. Faith will always be in the crucible.
 B. Christianity is validated by personal experience, the Scriptures, and the facts of history.

IV. Project for the Week
 A. Reread Galatians 3:1-14.
 B. Consider your own spiritual pilgrimage. Are you presently moving ahead? (Keep it up!) Are you in spiritual decline? (Beware!)
 C. Take whatever steps are necessary to help you move forward—confession, restitution, reaffirmation, fresh trust, and so on.
 D. Read Galatians 3:15-4:2 in preparation for our next study on "Why the Law?"

CIRCLES OF CONCERN
1974-1975

Purpose: Circles of Concern exist to provide a small group experience for the members of the Whittier Area Baptist Fellowship. In a church of moderate size it is necessary to meet in smaller groupings so as to minister to one another. Through study, sharing, and socializing we hope to better understand what it means to "weep with those who weep" and "rejoice with those who rejoice." Circles are successful to the degree that they foster caring for one another. Each circle is intended to become an intimate concerned community, namely, a church within the church.

RESPONSIBILITIES OF CIRCLE LEADERS

1. Be a caring person.
2. Pray for each member of the circle at least once a week.
3. Lead the studies and socials.
4. Keep in regular contact with all members. Phone regarding circle gatherings, and encourage participation in worship, Sunday school, and other church-related opportunities
5. Visit sick and delinquent members.
6. Communicate needs to the church staff.

CALENDAR

Leaders' Meetings		Circle Study		Social
Wednesday, Sept. 4	(7:00-8:30)	Wednesday, Sept. 11	(7:00-8:30)	October
Wednesday, Nov. 6	(7:00-8:30)	Wednesday, Nov. 13	(7:00-8:30)	December
Wednesday, Jan. 8	(7:00-8:30)	Wednesday, Jan. 15	(7:00-8:30)	February
Wednesday, March 5	(7:00-8:30)	Wednesday, March 12	(7:00-8:30)	April
Wednesday, May 7	(7:00-8:30)	Wednesday, May 14	(7:00-8:30)	June

Meeting No. 1
CIRCLES OF CONCERN
September 11, 1974

1. Create a congenial environment—chairs in a circle, appropriate sacred music, name tags for everyone (first name in large letters).
2. Introduce the circle idea. Focus upon the *concern* element. If we want to *care* for one another, it will be necessary that we *share* with one another.
3. Self-introductions. Have each person write three things on a paper: name, occupation, what I would like to see happen to me this year through our circle. These should be shared with the group and then collected by the leader.
4. Read 1 John 1. Read around the circle, one verse per person.
5. Ask the group to define *fellowship* (Koinonia).
   What, according to the text, is necessary if we are to have fellowship with God? With one another?
   What steps can we take tonight to encourage our fellowship?
6. Solicit prayer requests, particularly personal needs of the group.
7. Conclude with a short period of prayer (possibly conversational prayer).
8. Discuss an October social (have some ideas to "prime the pump").

CIRCLES OF CONCERN
1975-76

The Circles of Concern are a unique ministry within the Whittier Area Baptist Fellowship. These Circles of Concern are mini-Christian communities organized to provide a more meaningful experience in a "caring" and "sharing" atmosphere.

Objectives of the Circles of Concern:
1. To facilitate constructive dialogue and share common family experiences
2. To encourage each Christian in the circle to face and resolve the conflicts found in daily living
3. To improve their skills of relating to one another
4. To strengthen their respect for one another as well as themselves
5. To fortify each member of the group in order to stand fast in the Lord

Responsibilities of Leader:
1. Lead the Bible study and discussion sessions
2. Attend staff meetings every other month
3. Notify co-leader in case of absence from group

Responsibilities of Co-leader:
1. Make arrangements for meetings
2. Contact members to be present, refreshments, and so on
3. Fill in when leader is absent

CALENDAR
1975-1976

Leaders Meeting	Family Home Fellowship	Adult Growth Group Church Session
Sept. 24	Oct. 1	Nov. 5
Nov. 26	Dec. 3	Jan. 7
Jan. 28	Feb. 4	Mar. 3
Mar. 31	Apr. 7	May 5
May 26	Jun. 2	

Time of Meetings: 7:00-8:30 P.M.

CIRCLE OF CONCERN
October 1, 1975

I. Emphasis: "The Member . . . Care One for Another" (1 Cor. 12:25)

II. Objective: To facilitate constructive dialogue and share common family experience

III. Goal: Fellowship

IV. Procedure
   A. Provide a seating situation where most of the members can see one another's faces.
   B. Introductions
      1. Introduce yourself and family, your role in the circle.
      2. Go around the room and have each person give his or her name, what he or she would like to receive from being in a circle this year. They could indicate why they chose this group to be in.
   C. Lesson
      1. Read Acts 2:41-47.
      2. Project
         a. Adults: Draw a picture or write a brief poem of what *fellowship* says to you.
         b. Children: Draw a picture of what *fellowship* means to you.
      3. Share results of the project.
      4. Leader summarize ways the members can care and share this year.
      5. Prayer: A time of caring and sharing for one another.
   D. Application
      1. As a circle of concern, prayerfully seek out one family (or person) in WABF to join your circle.
      2. Share with one missionary your concern for his or her welfare by mail.